From

The Women's Press Ltd
34 Great Sutton Street, London EC1V 0DX

Maria Marcone   *Photo: Ramosini Bari*

Maria Marcone was born in Foggia, south Italy, where she trained
as a teacher. She is now living in Bari, where she works on scripts
for radio and television.

She has won numerous prizes for her novels, short stories and
poetry. *Analisi in Famiglia*, her fourth novel, won first prize in the
Villa San Giovanni Prize, category 'Problems of women in the
south'; was shortlisted for the Viareggio Prize in 1977 and the Maria
Marangelli Prize in 1979; and has been translated into Swedish,
French, German, Dutch and Spanish. It is the first of her books to
be translated into English. The RAI television film adapted from
the novel has been shown internationally.

MARIA MARCONE

A Woman and her Family

Translated from the Italian by
Etain Addey

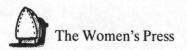 The Women's Press

First published in Great Britain by
The Women's Press Limited 1987
A member of the Namara Group
34 Great Sutton Street, London EC1V 0DX

First published in Italy under the title *Analisi in Famiglia* by
Giangiacomo Feltrinelli Editore, Milan, 1977

British Library Cataloguing in Publication Data

Marcone, Maria
 A Woman and her family
 I. Title   II. Analisi in Famiglia.
 853'.914 [F]   PQ4873.A69224/*English*

 ISBN 0–7043–5031–9
 ISBN 0–7043–4056–9 Pbk

Typeset by MC Typeset Ltd, Chatham, Kent
Printed and bound by Hazell Watson & Viney Ltd,
Aylesbury, Buckinghamshire

Contents

Case Histories

Franco – a born patriarch, a man in a state of permanent strategic retreat from life bar the odd reappearance which always meets with resounding failure. Forty-five years old, a typical Mediterranean look about him, and hair that is fast receding. He is really a school teacher, but for the past three years he's been invigilating in a lengthy competitive examination for teaching posts which looks as if it will never come to an end. This job sometimes takes him up to the capital, to his great relief and ours.

All the rest of his time he dedicates to his political party, where he acts as a sort of lackey. Occasionally he manages to do some real favour for one of the many have-nots who come asking him to use his influence with the people who really count. He is so excessively honest that he has never got anywhere careerwise. He uses his honesty for his self-appointed task of Censor and Reformer.

He'd never had the slightest suspicion that a husband might behave differently from the millions of examples he saw around him. It was only when his role began to fall apart that he was forced to face up to this idea. And of course he was quite sure that he was the best of fathers and had all the whys and wherefores clear in his own mind. Even when he began to see less clearly and realised it might be necessary to behave differently, he still couldn't grasp how to be different, or when, or what the aim of it might be.

Because his aim was to turn his children into two perfect, well trained puppets, ready to fit into a respectable niche in society. And, if at all possible, he'd have liked them to be winners, so they could make the losers pay – unlike himself; he had been obliged to fit in quietly as an underdog. He was very hurt when he saw that, as soon as his children achieved any sort of independence, they resolutely chose the losing side and now do nothing but lose. And he can't forgive me for joining the rebellion instead of helping him in the good work.

Marta is sixteen, with a great mop of hair and big, deep, gentle eyes. She is all fire – an erupting volcano. All moods and situations are grist to her mill. She leaps in wherever the ideological battle rages most fiercely, always on the lookout for anything that seems better, different, more authentic, with which to quench her thirst for truth. She plays the guitar and has such a powerful voice, so sweet and vital, that it makes you tremble. An instinctive anarchist, there can be no discussion about her convictions: she asserts them with violent finality. As far as she is concerned, her father and I have not understood a thing. Nevertheless, she likes her father's earthy vitality and she enjoys talking to me and exchanging ideas, so long as it's on equal terms.

Marco, at fourteen and a half, has a beard and long, black hair and a very sweet, clear look in his eyes. A few months ago his appearance cost him the attentions of two young neo-fascist thugs on the lookout for easy victories. As a matter of fact, although he is beginning to question things, he has kept his distance so far from militant politics. He is still taken up with his own problems, feeling his way towards a personal identity after the collapse of his father model and his own rejection of the stereotype male behaviour he sees everywhere, both in adult society and amongst his peers. We nicknamed this typical male 'Lops', after the surname of the first boy of this kind that Marco had anything to do with. He belonged to a local species of street kid, full of native wit, quick with his fists, foul-mouthed and sacrilegious, scornful of any culture except his own subculture, supposed repository of genuine popular wisdom, swaggering and sure of himself and his ability to survive anything, full of bad habits; a real man who sees women as something to screw – if they won't give in they'll end up as skivvies, dishing up a baby a year; if they lie still, they're fucking whores.

Marco was the defenceless child of parents who had lost this easy sense of security and so his first contact with this

2

species was traumatic. He tried to survive by rejecting his own identity and assuming theirs. It gave him a chance to flex his muscles and find the strength to escape his father's domination. Then he retraced his steps a bit and now he has a love – hate relationship with the street boys. He is still searching through the smoking ruins for his real identity. Often he's overcome by all kinds of groundless fears which sometimes emerge as pains in some part of his body or other. Or else the terrors are transformed into fanatical attachment to a beloved object such as the new sound system, bought recently at a reasonable price – still a month's salary to us. Lately Marco has changed: he is less emotional and instinctive in his reactions and more thoughtful and critical. Sometimes he comes out with extraordinarily well-balanced and moderate opinions that are quite unexpected in someone still so prone to violent ups and downs.

Finally there's myself. Forty-five, worn out by the toil and struggle of daily existence, torn between all my roles: housemaid, short-order cook, wife in search of new ways to love and be loved (a constant battleground), mother, confidante, psychologist, sociologist and teacher at odds with the official school system. A teacher who tries to make her work useful for her pupils, but uncertain as to her success. A human being searching for an identity, who aspires to become a fully developed person before dying as a larva. A woman who wants to express her real self to other people, but who lacks the space and often feels herself suffocating and collapsing beneath all the difficulties.

We don't have many real friends, in the sense of people we see often and in whom we can confide. Marta's friends are passionately loved and valued, but their turnover is fast. Marco has had one good friend since early childhood – Luciano, a rare boy indeed. He has a brother damaged by meningitis, and this experience of trouble in the family makes him able to respond easily to my son's funny ways. From the age of six, Marco and Luciano have shared their games, their interests – and now they share the desire to have a girl in their arms.

Franco too has only one real friend. He is a friend of mine as well, although there is that subtle barrier that divides

3

friends of the opposite sex. Giovanni is Franco's refuge. He is an eccentric, gifted person, torn by deep unhealed wounds that date back to early childhood. He is a melting pot of irreconcilable contradictions: beast and angel; unsatisfied, repressed sexuality and great ideological aspirations towards some non-existent world. In the wider sense of the word, of course, Franco has a vast number of friends.

I have very few people that I see often. But perhaps I have more real friends. Wanda and I have been friends since we were at infant school. She was my companion in the days when my mind was really fertile. She is a part of me, and even though distance now prevents us from keeping up with each other's lives, we are both involved in the search for our real selves.

Nora was the friend of my student days; years later I found her immersed in her own family tragedy. I go to see her often in the hope of finding in her weary eyes some sign of the fire she possessed when I first knew her. Sometimes it flares up from under the ashes where it's buried.

Annuccia I met a few years ago, when she was still full of life and revolutionary energy, full of fight and faith. She seemed to me then stronger and more confident than I was, and that is what I liked in her. Now I am shocked to see her surrendering to circumstances, bent under the weight of routine, resigned to the worst, forgetful of herself, empty, swallowed up by the routine of school and family, locked into a sacrificing-mother/demanding-son relationship with her husband and yet submissive to her male patriarch.

Finally there's Emilia, whom I met recently – fished out of the grey sea of a provincial school like a pearl. My relationship with her is beautiful – warm, but sad as well, because she too is suffocated by her family. And she is even more of a prisoner than I am to the rules and rituals of respectable society. But her spirit is alive, and I like this vitality; I like the way she has of hanging on through thick and thin.

Then, on the sidelines, there are our supervisors – my relations and Franco's. They are merciless and unbending judges of our deviations from the norm and they are only held at bay by our own efforts. At one time they were far more determined and stubborn in their defence of the system which we questioned and criticised. Now they are somewhat resigned to our obstinacy in going our own way: it is obvious to them that we intend to follow our path even if it brings us to the very edge of the precipice.

The sole exception is my mother. Every so often she breaks through our carefully erected barrier. She never gives up: she returns time and time again with the indomitable strength of a matriarch who feels it her duty to watch over her prodigal daughter. If necessary she will brave storms and dangers to rescue me *in extremis*, because nothing will convince her that I am not horribly unhappy. She sees me as a defenceless and passive victim in the hands of three wicked, selfish monsters who are slowly bleeding me to death. There is no way of getting it across to her that not only am I very much alive, but that I have a most interesting life of my own, which I would not change for that of any other woman. She can't see that although I suffer, I am also in the process of freeing myself gradually from bonds that were forced on me long ago. The premises for my future slavery were established under the guise of love when I was a small child. She thinks my slavery began with my marriage – an institution she abhors because of her own personal experience of it. She claims that if only I'd stayed at home, I should have been free to live as I wished. She won't admit that when I met Franco I felt it was a liberation, even if it turned out to be only the illusion of freedom. The fact is that when I was at home I was everybody's slave for the very reason that I was 'free' – free from ties of my own – so that everybody used me as and when they needed me, draining all my energies without recharging me, even though they gave me reasonable doses of their affection and respect.

The extent to which I was a slave at home can easily be judged by the feeling of betrayal that my departure produced in my mother, even though my flight was consecrated by marriage to Franco. For years she saw Franco as a thief who had stolen her most valuable possession – valuable because she had invested a great deal in it. How can I explain to her that if I had not escaped from the comfortable, paralysing family life, I should very soon have ended up a dried larva, going through a series of automatic actions, dragging out an existence of unrewarding duties with no life-giving content to them?

In the eyes of my mother, who has only seen my married life from the outside, my encounter with Franco was a terrible mistake, a calamity. And it's no use my trying to make her see that for me, as I was then, it was the only possible encounter. I can't explain that, in spite of everything, Franco and I are growing – yes, growing, even at our age, when most people have long ceased to grow, and that as we become more mature we are happier than ever to be together. 'Well, in that case you must have been sick too,' she concludes, and by 'sick' she means anyone who is not 'normal', anyone who seeks an authentic, independent life away from all the preconceived and preordained rules. This is diametrically opposed to my own view: I fight shy of any rule or precept that I haven't tried out myself and made my own. I look around me and I see that most people are no more than puppets, moved by strings that disappear back into the mists of time. The puppets move in lines, they wear blinkers: they will never look truth in the face, the truth that I'm still after and that now begins to emerge before me, a little at a time. Even these fragments of truth more than repay me for all the struggles I sustained on the way. Poor mother, she seems far away now, wrapped up in her unquestioning certainties. And I feel sorry for her, too – perhaps more than she does for me.

Maybe this is why recently, although I still feel affection for her (indeed a deeper and purer affection, as if between two innocents), the encounter with my origins no longer produces the same feelings in me. Now at last the umbilical cord has really withered and can no longer feed me with its life-giving fluid. Now I really am an adult being, no longer a creature born of another, but a living, self-sufficient being ready to live that short autonomous life that is the lot of transient humanity. It was a hard-won achievement: I revel in it with a sense of awareness but also with astonishment. Because when I look at the people who pass me in the street or who walk alongside me, all I see are umbilical cords. The cords are rotten and withered but the people continue to carry them around – as if they are afraid to cut them in case such a bold move might strike them to the ground. Especially people of my generation.

But then I see all the young kids confidently killing off their mothers and fathers as fast as they can, sustained by their theories yet still hampered by guilt and by the curses gasped out in their parents' dying breaths. And the parents themselves seem to cling to those umbilical relationships with a sort of desperate survival instinct. Unable to lead real adult lives themselves, they are terrified in case their children might learn to do so. It is almost as if they see this search for new lifestyles and new values as the sin which got Adam and Eve thrown out of Paradise – the original sin, the search which set Ulysses off on his travels past the Pillars of Hercules. And so they scream threats and warnings, with the result that many young people fall by the wayside and clamber back up their umbilical cords until they find a place where the cord hasn't dried up altogether. And there they stay, paralysed and motionless, for ever.

I will do my very best not to stand in the way of my children when they try to cut their cords. I will let them go off on the great, unique adventure of life in that small space afforded by human existence, a space which can pan out to infinity or fill the brief span of a sunlit morning. Even if it costs me the disapproval of 'respectable' folk – family, school, society at large – who all condemn me as a bad educator and a bad mother: so bad as to be almost perverted.

I am glad that I am: it's my starting point in my search for truth and my own freedom. And yet it's not easy to get even this far, just to the starting point. Not everyone is lucky enough to reach it. A great many factors played their part: circumstances, a situation that seemed to have no way out, the pain I endured for years, the stubborn, desperate need to break through it all, to bite clean through the bonds, maybe just good luck too – or bad luck, depending on how you look at it. You land up on a distant shore – and from this shore you can see a palm-fringed island, far away on the horizon. The island is still unexplored, and who knows what monsters may lurk there – perhaps even more frightening monsters than those you've overcome so far.

7

Now I am going to try and retrace my steps, so as to get things into perspective. Perhaps I will free myself from the troublesome ghosts of the past which – though they no longer possess me – still return to haunt my mind, assuming the faces of those around me. I won't follow any particular time sequence. I will let the ghosts visit me as they wish, beginning at the point which is deepest and furthest back in my memory, where the living creature had almost ceased to breathe.

Analysis of a Family

When I first felt the need to unravel the mess my life was in, I'd been living for years in a state of such wretchedness that I was the very image of lost hope. This need to get at least some things sorted out roused me. It was not so much my sense of survival which emerged – that had long since turned into mere passive resistance – but my maternal instinct, because I realised that I had to rescue my son, who was in danger. I had to reach out and drag him out of the quicksands that were sucking him down.

Our lives were the same dreary lives that all city people lead nowadays, locked into the routine of work and family. Although we lacked any really constructive response to them, we had all the usual problems of family life in an urban context: working parents, small children to take to school or to the park for fresh air and to protect from all the dangers of the street, not enough time, not enough space, a family budget that floundered at the least lapse in sensible management, difficult relationships with the extended family who 'never see enough of us', superficial relationships with neighbours and friends.

In those days Franco was absolute lord and master of our lives, ruthlessly controlling our every move, and the difficult circumstances surrounding the early days of our marriage made him feel all the more justified in this attitude. At the beginning of our married life we had lived in my home town, and we had been involved in a whole series of misguided enterprises there, organised by my younger brothers. I had found the situation very frustrating, and finally the ups and downs and misunderstandings persuaded me to give in and follow Franco back to his native city, where we now live, and where it seemed that everything might take a turn for the better.

But Franco was disappointed by the circle he found here, so different from that of his university days and made up of ageing socialists who had been pushed aside by the new, ruthless young leftists on their way up. He couldn't bring himself to leave his own political party, which meant so much to him and which was still associated in his mind with the wholehearted political struggles of his youth. He was pushed from behind by his own family with their laborious middle-class aspirations, and he felt frustrated at coming home without having made it financially, without even the price of a home to live in – with nothing, in fact, but his own modest salary and his wife's. Another source of bitterness was the dwindling prestige of the teaching profession, a profession which had seemed respectable and socially desirable to Franco when he had set out to get his degree. He had come up against all the class prejudice that any working-class boy met in the academic world at that time, and his road to teaching qualifications had been a hard one, beset with obstacles.

And here was I, the only person to whom he could pour out his fury and indignation, the perfect target, because I belonged to the hated Italian middle class to which he aspired so desperately. He hadn't the courage to soil his pristine sense of honour by playing the usual power games in the outside world – the only way to prove oneself smart enough to join the middle-class club. And he took it out on me, accusing me of being not a hardworking teacher trying to do a good job, dutiful mother, careful housekeeper, health-conscious cook and maid-of-all-work, but only the daughter of a well-to-do family which had dissipated his money and ruined his reputation in shady business deals. He also cursed me for bringing him a dowry consisting of nothing but furniture and household goods instead of money to buy a house – the one possession that was absolutely vital as a first step up the social ladder, crowded as it was in those years with millions of Italians jostling for a foothold during the economic boom. He accused me of not having fought hard enough to ensure for ourselves and our children the lifestyle that my family's social standing should have made possible. He ignored the fact that my family consisted of a widow and three unemployed sons, whose only real fault lay in their inability to turn to good account the little money that my mother had inherited from her father – actually two old houses which, once sold and the death duties paid, yielded a paltry sum. But when Franco talked about my family, he really meant my grandparents, whom he had met when we were engaged to be married. It was they who had given him the impression of affluence, which was in reality already declining and by then was represented by no more than a lavish and plentiful table, rendered even more glamorous by my grandmother's famous cooking. Franco, lean and under-nourished from years of going without, and permanently ravenous, used to sit down at that table and eat himself to a standstill, and my well-meaning grandmother, who couldn't bear to think of her favourite granddaughter marrying a half-starved waif, did her best to fatten him up. But above all, when Franco mentioned my family, he was referring to my uncle, a real old Scrooge who had built up a fortune from a small inheritance by racking his brains to think up every financial deal in the book. Now he kept watch over his fortune like an anxious old miser, and suffered terrible liverish attacks each time it seemed threatened by his relations or by occasional adverse circumstances.

I never did see what my uncle had to do with me. Anyway, I was the one who paid for all the wicked speculations of the hated Italian middle class, and all the while I was quietly and uncomplainingly working away at my own tasks.

I didn't complain because I felt guilty for being a member of the middle class, even though I had hated it myself and had done my best – as far as I could from the inside – to separate and distance myself from it. But the mental confusion that Franco's persecution created in me made it impossible for me to see myself as separate from my family. I knew I was different, but then I only knew it in theory, because in practice I had begun to identify myself with them so as to hang on to some sort of identity, now that I felt so completely crushed and annihilated as an individual.

Our sex life, which had never been wonderful, began to go

downhill fast. Franco grabbed me whenever he felt like it without so much as a by-your-leave, threw me around like a sack of potatoes, and did brutal, sadistic things to me as the whim took him; then left me where I lay, battered and motionless, brooding like a wounded animal, unable to defend myself or rebel. It couldn't even have been masochism, because I hadn't the slightest feeling of collusion in the brutalising, crushing process.

Anyone, indeed, who watched me as I went about my day's work would have thought me the very picture of a perfect wife and mother; they would even have thought me a woman with a full and satisfying life. In the morning I left the children and the house in the hands of a daily help, whose main job was to look after the children, wash and dress them, give them breakfast and spend time with them, doing a bit of housework if and when she got the time, until I came home from school. And I managed to build up a satisfying and – for those days – enlightened relationship with my secondary school pupils.

On my way home I did the shopping, and I would come in laden down with bags. The daily help would go off, and I would make lunch for the two children, who were then three and four and a half. I sat them up at the kitchen table, and I sat between them and fed them – a spoonful each, a spoon in each hand, and they opened their little round mouths eagerly and then chewed, their fat soft cheeks moving rhythmically. I told them fairy stories, mostly made up on the spur of the moment and going on from where we'd stopped the day before, without my having any idea how the story would end. Sometimes they would be true stories about famous people, or else about ordinary folk, or about nature, how the planets and stars were formed, about the lives of plants and animals, especially those amazing prehistoric animals, so terrifying and huge. And my small listeners asked me who made all these extraordinary things, and who made the creator, and why this creator, who I said knew everything, had invented creatures so big and stupid that they couldn't survive at all.

They ate so happily and it was the one moment in the day that I enjoyed, which no amount of oppression could spoil for me. It was a time when I felt that I was not only

nourishing my children's bodies, but also, and more impor-
tantly their minds. I was completely relaxed and at ease, free
to communicate to them all the things I'd studied and
thought about over the years. Then I cooked lunch for my
husband. I didn't so much eat with him as serve him while he
ate and read the newspaper. He took no notice of me except
to ask if the children had eaten, if they were constipated or
not, if they had caught colds, or if anything untoward had
happened to them – in which case I was the one at fault
because I was such a wicked and unnatural mother. Then
Franco would use me as his scapegoat, heaping on my head
all the anxieties he – as a loving father – felt. When I had
finished the housework I used to take the children out to get
some fresh air – in winter that means by three o'clock – and
as we went downstairs I'd hear Franco shouting – not the
words of an affectionate husband, but a great flow of stern
and peremptory threats. By now I was so used to them, I
hardly heard them any more because he'd been shouting the
same things after me ever since I first took the children out,
as babies in their prams.

It went like this, 'You watch those children! If you let
anything happen to them – even a scratch or a tumble, I'll kill
you.' I'd get out into the freedom of the open air, but those
offensive words would ring in my ears, and I never managed
to feel relaxed and at ease like the other mothers I saw in the
park, who chatted happily to each other, or knitted away
while their children frolicked about on the grass with their
balls, their skates, their bicycles, and all sorts of other toys
that my children were not allowed to have. My children were
supposed to stay in a restricted space right near me, and I
was supposed to watch them all the time, without ever taking
my eyes off them. So I could never make friends with
anyone, nor could I let the children do so, because that
would have involved a completely different approach to life –
one that was forbidden us. We watched everyone else getting
on with life instead of living ourselves, and we felt different
and left out, as if we were some strange species from another
planet.

Marta was an exuberant little girl, and she still managed to
have fun in her own way, but Marco was already frozen with

fear, because all through his babyhood he'd been told over and over again not to move too much. The excuse was that he had a slight tendency to inguinal and umbilical hernia, although this was held in check by a little belt, and lately he'd begun to have a touch of bronchial asthma, and this gave his father yet another excuse for endless precautions and restrictions. It all seemed to me a bit too much and I thought all the fussing made things worse, but then I was a bad and irresponsible mother, so my views counted for less than nothing. I don't know whether the children felt any sense of freedom in that tiny little bit of open space that they were allowed. It made me suffer; it made me feel like a dim, mangy old dog with no right even to exist or to reproduce.

By the time I got home, Franco would be back from visiting his mother. He went to see her every day, and for some reason I was always the subject of their conversation, and I could tell from the angry look on Franco's face how kindly their comments about me must have been.

I think the main thing that my mother-in-law reproached her son with was not getting a house out of my parents. It was a well established tradition in Bari for the bride to bring with her a home in exchange for the privilege of being married. Moreover, he'd chosen a woman from another area, whose ways were alien to good Bari society. Worse still, he'd actually picked a woman from Foggia, despite the bad name the women there had – real witches, ugly and crafty as shrews and, in this particular case, too much of a lady for their simple tastes.

These were the sort of comments which Franco heard every day, as well as more specific criticisms of anything I said or did to try and get them to accept me. No wonder that when Franco came back from these pilgrimages to his parents he saw me through their eyes – and they were stern and pitiless eyes, with no flicker of human feeling in them, let alone love or respect. He would unleash a hail of accusations at me, all about my family: they had never loved me, they had done absolutely nothing to help our married life, and so on and so on. He would wind up by enjoining me to watch those children, to give them a glycerine suppository if they were constipated, not to let them get into draughts, not to let them fall down or get overheated, on pain of death, and then he'd be off to see his friends at the local party headquarters.

And I would spend the rest of the day alone, cut off from the outside world, playing with the children, listening to music with them, drawing or making plasticine dollies, telling them stories at suppertime, rocking them for hours when I put them to bed, singing to them quietly – maybe a little sadly too; making up the words and tunes, so that instead of going to sleep they'd lie warm and snug in the dark with their eyes wide open. Meanwhile my husband had come home. He would eat, and while he ate he watched television. He never asked me if I'd already eaten. As a matter of fact I used to eat almost furtively in those days, like someone who knows the food is stolen and that they've no right to eat it at all.

That's how low I had sunk. I no longer read, or took any interest in the news, I lead a completely isolated life. I was just a drudge and I hated myself.

In the spring I took Marta to a nuns' nursery school – the only one that Franco, the revolutionary, said he trusted. I hoped that at least she'd have more space to move in there, and it did seem to be so. But I would come home from work to find Marco curled up in the corner of an armchair, with a sad little face and a tummy ache. I would take him to the park, if we had time, and then we'd go and pick up his sister. One morning I noticed, with a sense of shock, how fearful he'd become. I was sitting on a stone bench in the park, and Marco was in my lap with his feet stretched out along the bench. Another mother came and sat down next to me, with a child about the same age as mine – and her child immediately held out his chubby arms and smiled at Marco. Marco was terrified and hid his face in my arms, trembling with fright, and I couldn't do anything with him – I had to carry him away, apologising to the other woman, who looked astonished. I told her he'd been ill, cooped up in the house for days, and that he probably wasn't really better yet. But I knew very well that the real explanation was quite different.

As soon as Marco saw his sister he forgot his aches and pains, because Marta's cheerful noise made him laugh. The one positive thing which left me some feeling of self-respect was the happy relationship which I'd managed to create between my two children. I had been careful right from the start to be equally loving and caring with both of them, and to encourage their love and affection for each other, so that after every fight they'd always kiss each other and make it up – and that used to fill my heart with joy.

But soon this last source of self-respect disappeared: now that Marta spent some time away from the family, she became more independent and outgoing, and this didn't fit in at all with the reign of terror which prevailed in our house. During the same period Marco had suffered a real attack of asthma – not serious, but bad enough to rekindle his father's overanxiousness and give him an excuse to restrict Marco's life even further, to the point where only complete paralysis would really have satisfied him.

In my role as slave-cum-prison-guard I found it harder and harder to reconcile the children's exuberant vitality with my orders to keep them still, and so I used to take it out on Marta, who was the livelier one, and if she took no notice of me, I would raise my hand to slap her. And then I would get mad when she responded by laughing in my face, full of fun and high spirits. I realised I'd hit rock bottom; I was just like any silly, hysterical woman with no understanding of child psychology; I was no more than the larval form of the woman and mother I wanted to be – I was really disgusting. I couldn't seem to find any inspiration or help in the memories of my father, though he had been a source of strength for years; I couldn't turn to my mother, who already suffered torments over me without the least idea of the level to which I'd really sunk. Thus, adrift and alone, I reached the point where I fell ill.

The first symptoms appeared when I was at school. I was in the middle of a lesson, when suddenly I felt such a sense of anguish mounting inside me that I could hardly breathe. My heart was racing, and then all at once everything went black, a steel vice seemed to grip my heart, and a deadly cold crept up my limbs. Everyone ran to help me, and I was sent home accompanied by two worried colleagues. Someone phoned Franco and he came rushing home, alarmed. But I was already beginning to feel better, the weight in my chest was lifting and the blood seemed to flow back into my veins and warm me. I said quickly that I felt fine; I was ashamed to let Franco see me ill. And sure enough, Franco was already pacing up and down at the foot of my bed, grumbling that this was all he needed, an invalid wife, that he was the most unfortunate man alive, and that all his friends had married proper wives, full of health and wealth. This was enough to get me out of bed and back to the grindstone, feeling more humiliated and disheartened than ever.

But these attacks became more and more frequent, and they often happened in the mornings, at school. I'm sure there were two good, though unconscious, reasons for this. First, I no longer thought I was equal to the job. My self-esteem had fallen so low that I felt I had nothing to offer the kids I had to teach – and they, of course, expected something from me – I'm not sure exactly what. Second, even though I was still rather an outsider in that environment, it was the one place where I found some semblance of human solidarity and tolerance, and so I must have felt it was safe to be ill there. I never told Franco about these episodes if I could possibly help it.

I still didn't know many people in Bari and I felt alone in my predicament. The only thing Franco did to help was to give me the address of a GP, an old friend of the family, the sort of overworked doctor who never thinks anyone is seriously ill unless they are actually dying, and who sees women as a subspecies good for nothing except love-making and child-bearing. He examined me and said there was nothing really wrong with me, and that the trouble with women is that we don't have enough babies nowadays and so our heads are full of silly fancies.

I used to phone Nora up, and pour it all out into her sympathetic ear. She was pregnant at the time, so she had some respite from her usual nightmarish routine. Her story was no better than mine: though a graduate, she was only the daughter of a farm labourer, so her marriage to a judge was considered rather too presumptuous. In order to compensate for her own comparatively low status, she had been expected to earn a sort of post-wedding dowry by doing private lessons as well as the housework and her ordinary teaching job. She was permanently exhausted, and her first

17

baby was stillborn.

Nora would comfort me, and then, because her husband Mattia liked me too, having met me on the odd occasion when I'd managed to visit them and find the energy to talk, they both took to coming round in the evenings, when the children were in bed, and talking to me about my problems. They gave me the courage to let some of my feelings rise to the surface from under the weight of oppression, and I managed a timid attempt at rebellion.

Thus one day I found myself with a pen in my hand, writing, searching for an identity somewhere in my past – maybe in the love my father had shown me, or in the long discussions I used to have with Wanda; perhaps in the ideals I'd had once, or even in the old dreams of glory. From all this grew my first book. It had no real depth of perception, no real sense of awareness, and perhaps its only virtue lay in the simplicity of its rather dreamlike story. I rose a little in Franco's estimation after this, because he had a great respect for anything literary.

He offered to act as my secretary, to type out the manuscript and send it round the publishers for me. Encouraged by Franco, who suddenly decided that I ought to have space for my writing, I wrote several short stories and got them accepted for publication. Franco now began to make love to me with a little more affection, though he still ignored my need for any satisfaction. He treated me more like a person again, chatting away about publishers and critics, and about my writing. I let him talk, but it offended me: why did he have to use such discussions as a substitute for love talk?

The printed book and my name in the press made a great impression on Franco, and he began to treat me like an idol to be revered. This made me uncomfortable because I didn't feel I'd done anything so very extraordinary, and also because he'd begun to build this new activity of mine into a barrier between the children and me; I never meant it to interfere with our relationship. When he came in with the post, he'd call the children so they could see and hear what people were saying about me. I would protest, because I was sure they weren't really interested, but he took no notice. He thought they ought to be impressed to hear what people had to say about their mother. Perhaps he felt he was making up for all the scorn he'd poured on me in front of them. He could certainly see the results of this for himself, because by this time the children ordered me around as if I were their personal slave.

I didn't feel guilty about the children. It didn't seem to me that I was depriving them of my time or attention. But Franco's family began to reproach me with this, especially his father, a true patriarch who believed that a married woman's place is in the home with her children. Even an outside job seemed to him a loss rather than an extra salary, because then someone has to be paid to do some of her housework and childcare; so my father-in-law had plenty to say about me, because I taught, and had domestic help, and now I even spent time writing as well. He criticised my housekeeping – the place was too messy and untidy. He criticised the way I brought up the children – he thought their lack of freedom was designed to save me time and trouble, and he didn't seem to understand that it was Franco who laid down strict rules for their behaviour. Both my in-laws complained that I didn't visit them often enough. I would have gone there more frequently had not Franco forbidden me to do so: he didn't like me going out. So when Franco went on his own daily visit to his parents, he got a whole fresh set of criticisms on the subject of me, and he used to come home just as cross as ever, full of reproach and condemnation, and very displeased indeed that he'd married a woman like me, who gave him such a lot of trouble.

Maybe he was right, maybe it was like that, maybe it was all my fault for being different, and for having unusual interests compared with most women: I certainly found it hard to take an interest in the talk I heard from colleagues and relations when they started on about clothes, handbags, furniture, cleaning fluids, recipes, parties and official receptions. If they dreamed dreams, they were all of fur coats and jewellery, holiday villas by the sea or in the mountains, sports cars, fabulous trips and so on. Yes, I was different: my universe was made up of the things of nature, of feelings and ideas and reflections on the world and people – politics, in other words. I had begun to take notice of the outside world again, but I could see that the women I knew had no time for politics. They regarded politics as boring men's business, and they behaved as if the political decisions which men were making on their behalf had nothing to do with them and held no consequences for them. It was not so much the frustration of being different that got me down, as the stream of criticism I heard from the chorus of friends, relations and colleagues, who told me that I was right off the rails and that I would end up by wrecking my marriage and ruining my children.

And they were ruined! The first infant school teachers who were unlucky enough to be faced with my offspring saw at once that they were hopelessly different. At first the teachers said, with a note of admiration in their voices: 'They're born scholars! They know so much already!' But this difference quickly became a nuisance, something to be curbed – because these children talked back, jumped up and objected and offered opinions that were based on a sense of fairness, behaving like equals in a place where all the patterns of behaviour were irrational and prejudiced. And so they soon found themselves outcasts, frustrated and unable to com-municate or understand other people. It was hard for them to make friends, and they were lonely.

Marta, who was the more talkative and self-assertive of the two, managed to keep her head above water. She emerged as a leader, and found herself allies. But Marco was reticent and wary by nature, and he suffered a great deal in being different; he felt inferior and became introverted, solitary and irritable. Finally he, too, became ill. Only in his case it took the form of asthma, the anguish rising from the depths of this pent-up soul. I could see that what these children needed was space, light, and a more relaxed social life. They needed to get used to the open air, movement, other children, and I tried to do something to help them. I took them with me to look for a new flat. The three dark, suffocating rooms that we lived in at that time had been found for us by Franco's parents when we were moving to Bari, and I detested them – they were the very symbol of our oppression and slavery.

Together, the children and I chose a new flat. We liked it as soon as we saw it because it was full of air and sunlight and it was more spacious than the old apartment, and had more rooms. It had a cosy feel to it, and yet each member of the family would have more privacy too. We moved in with high hopes, as if this move would suffice to break the old routine that had become so unbearable.

And indeed, for a while we did have a sense of renewal in this flat. The children had a big, sunny room all to themselves, Franco had a little study befitting his professional dignity, and I got a larger and more comfortable kitchen in which to perform my humble tasks and my writing. There was also a cosy living room for us all, where we could entertain guests and where the children could play their wilder games as soon as their father left the house. In the evening we'd all watch television there in comfort. We also had wide balconies where the children could ride their bicycles – a recent purchase I had made, much to the delight of the children and the fury of my husband.

A full-length children's story of mine was published, and it was widely adopted for use in junior schools: once more I rose in Franco's estimation and he began to change his mind about the sort of wife he'd acquired. As usual, he thought it would make me happy to see how highly valued I was, but of course I was not at all pleased to see that I was no more than a commercial proposition to be exploited.

He was forever pressing me to accept offers from publishers. They all wanted me to turn out stories, any old stuff that they could rush on to the market fast, because at the time there was a great demand for children's books and the publishing trade was crawling with unscrupulous bookmongers on the make. But I felt reluctant to comply, and I would hesitate, play for time and eventually refuse, disappointing Franco and also the publishers, who gave me up as a bad job and decided I was too arrogant, too stupid and had no head for business: how like a woman not to grasp the requirements of the market.

My writing was just writing, it wasn't for a market: I was searching, delving within myself, and this unremunerative writing gave Franco no excuse to offer his family for this luxury occupation of mine, which only a lady of my pretensions could have dreamt up. To put a stop to the reproaches and the grumbling, I dismissed the daily help, who had at least done part of the housework for me. I did it all myself, with the pride of someone who's got two strong arms and can easily bear the weight of the whole world, if only they get their freedom in exchange. My writing didn't hurt anybody, because I did it in my free time, the time that other women use for making themselves beautiful, or for gossiping with their friends or going to parties.

But by this time my children had got it into their heads that I really was a bad and degenerate mother, having heard it said over and over again, and Marco in particular began to nurse a grudge against me and my writing. If I crossed him in the least little thing, he'd rush to seize my file of papers from the shelf – the papers he'd seen in my hands – and jump up and down on them in a furious rage. This reaction hurt me and I blamed Franco for it: I had begun to argue back and defend myself. Then, when I saw that Franco was immovable in his convictions, and incapable of any process of self-questioning or rethinking, I started actually attacking him. And once I got started, I attacked everything, rejecting his very personality – even though it was this I'd fallen in love with. He was like an unexplored jungle, just a mass of uncontrolled impulses and reactions; his refusal to discuss or analyse anything was total, and so was his conviction that he was the repository of all truth and justice. He also saw himself as the repository of all the rules of behaviour as established by tradition, and these rules were not to be changed or questioned. Thus, in his eyes, a husband is the rightful head of the household, and it is his duty to exercise his authority with any and every repressive and even violent means that society at large permits him. When I argued with him, he never came back at me with any reasons, he just repeated that I was the worst woman in the world, that now he understood how right his family were; he was a poor fool ever to have married a witch from Foggia, a poisonous serpent, a real bitch who only wanted her freedom so that she could jump into bed with someone else: in which case he really would kill me.

And with this threat he would slam the front door and go off to get his breath back at the party offices. Except that down there his frustration only increased, because things at the party had changed: gone was the old political breathing space and the sense of freedom, and recently Franco had been obliged to join the court of one of the new political climbers, who used Franco's famous reputation for honesty to cover up his own shady activities.

I attacked Franco for this as well, because until then his political integrity had been the one reason I still felt some respect for him. He had been instrumental in my own political education and consciousness, and it made me angry to see his ideals fall apart. All he seemed interested in was jumping on the bandwagon with all the other power-seekers; yet he didn't have the sort of drive you need to succeed and he always came home empty-handed – his loss of integrity didn't even pay off.

His reply to all this was that women don't understand anything, times had changed and as usual my reaction was off-beam: I ought to grasp the fact that nowadays if you aren't flexible, you're out. He began to preach compromise, and his integrity faded the nearer he drew to the climbers – those men who have always grown fat at the expense of the masses. His behaviour was incredibly contradictory: he hated the priests and nuns, yet he kissed the priests' hands and sent his children to the nuns' school; he detested the middle classes, yet he licked the feet of anyone, big or small, who was into good old exploitation. He even changed his mind about my old Uncle Scrooge, and said he was quite right to pile up the money, the system being what it was, and that my brothers, now they were over their initial mistakes and sailing in calmer financial waters, were good fellows.

Now there was nothing to keep us together. Our only tie was the two children we had together, and my writing, which he kindly transformed into manuscripts in the hope that one day they might enable him to claim a share in the good life whilst keeping his hands clean – culture was such a noble means to an end! This had become all the more desirable because the earning power of our teachers' salaries was falling so fast that our standard of living was almost beggarly.

On this slippery slope, I was hard put to find the equilibrium I sought so desperately. The state of my inner life showed in my frequent attacks of illness, which reappeared with all the usual symptoms, although at the time no one had diagnosed the problem for what it was. Since my economic value had risen, I allowed myself the luxury of a medical check-up with the best specialist in town. He examined me, did a set of tests and pronounced his verdict: I was suffering from mitral stenosis – a heart condition – and I required three-monthly check-ups. I didn't really have much faith in him, so I treated myself to a second opinion from another medical prima donna, who confirmed the diagnosis. I resigned myself to dying of the same disease that my father had died of. My mother was delighted to have such a wonderful vindication of her prophesies. She proclaimed that it was exactly what she'd always feared, that this had been her main reason for opposing my marriage to Franco, aware as she had been even then that a brief and bitter destiny awaited me, and that she herself would have to be on hand to care for me until the end came. Indeed she began to visit us far more often, and Franco stopped treating her as his number one enemy and began to gang up with her against this reprehensible wife of his. I was already guilty on so many counts, and now I was guilty of having a heart condition too, so that my services as a wife and mother must necessarily be substandard. Yet I worked without a break eighteen out of the twenty-four hours to get all my various jobs done, and my mother added a last fault to the list: I didn't even know how to take care of my looks or save myself work.

Now there was a double barrier between my children and me. First there was my writing, to which everyone objected with the exception of Franco, who was firmly convinced that it promised to fulfil all our hopes of economic advancement, even though these hopes were continually scotched by my refusal to bow to the demands of the system. And now there was my illness, which was held before the children – sometimes by their father or grandmother and sometimes by me – to make them see that it was time they helped around the house a bit like all their peers, at least to the extent of washing themselves, making the odd sandwich, getting on with their homework and keeping their toys and books tidy. Marco especially seemed to embody the same attitude of angry condemnation that he saw in his father, but he expressed it on a more instinctive level, with physical instead of verbal violence, and so there was endless kicking and punching.

He took no notice of me now, no matter what I said. It seemed as if his one desire was to do exactly the opposite of whatever I told him to do, and I couldn't help blaming this state of affairs on Franco. He replied that I didn't love the child and that I was too sharp with him. And that was probably true sometimes, but I didn't know how else to deal with Marco's unreasonable obstinacy. So Franco started taking his son off with him so as to stop me from treating him unfairly, and this made Marco all the more certain that I didn't care about him.

The other consequence, just as damaging, was the rift in the harmonious relationship between the two children. Together, the two of them had created an extraordinarily rich and original fantasy world. They made up stories and events just as I had done for years with them, and created games with dolls and characters of all sorts, so that a whole toyland took shape – or else they acted out the stories themselves in plays.

Perhaps at some stage Marco realised that his more dynamic and extrovert sister, with her ready creativity, had outstripped him, because she was older, and maybe the initial good feeling was lost in rivalry. Anyway, he emerged the frustrated and vengeful loser, ready at the slightest provocation to burst into a tantrum and kick his sister's toys to pieces. She would get furious with him, and I would feel obliged to come to her aid, but the peace I re-established between them became more and more precarious. By now, all my efforts only confirmed Marco's conviction that I was on his sister's side, and provoked more outbursts against her and against me too. I felt grieved and distressed and dissatisfied with the way I dealt with it all, and I blamed Franco for having put me in this hateful situation, for having stolen my son's love. I could see how it hurt Marco, I could see how his feelings of persecution oppressed him so that he could hardly maintain any friendship with his peers, who all appeared to him as sworn enemies. And his relationships with adults were no better: indeed he felt physically threatened by adults as well. It became so bad that it seemed as if he couldn't even share the bedroom with his sister any longer. I hesitated to separate them because I was afraid it might trigger a complete breakdown in their relationship. However, unforeseen circumstances and a period of extreme family tension induced me to separate them in spite of my feelings.

My mother had undergone a complicated operation, and when she was discharged from hospital she came to spend her convalescence at our house. In fact we found her already installed when we returned from the thermal springs where we'd taken Marco for his asthma. I had terrible feelings of guilt towards my mother because throughout her illness and her spells in various hospitals, I had been the only one of her children who'd failed to do anything for her; my three brothers and my aunt had done everything in their power to help, even taking it in turns to stay by her bedside night and day. I couldn't do anything because Franco, with the excuse that I had the children to look after, wouldn't let me. He said my family had given me nothing but trouble and didn't deserve anything from me. So I was torn between the terror of losing my mother, without even having shown her any love and care, and all my buried feelings of guilt which now rose to the surface with renewed stirrings of love and hate. I was near breaking point, and I would collapse in floods of secret tears, but I couldn't pull myself together sufficiently to insist on my right to help my mother. My only act of bravery was to leave the keys of the house with my aunt so that she could take my mother there when she came out of hospital. While we were away I tried on a hundred different occasions to break the news to Franco, but I was so bogged down in the increasingly difficult relationship with him and the children that I never found the courage to do so. I was in such a state that I used to burst into tears even when my husband was around. It disgusted him to see me crying for my mother: he thought such exaggerated misery was unworthy of a strong woman like me. But I was crying bitter tears for my slave-like position: I didn't dare tell about the keys to the house – I knew what sort of reaction I could expect from Franco when he found out, and so all I could hope was that my mother would die and never come out of the hospital at all. Then I felt sorrier for my mother than I'd ever felt in my life, because while she might expect her daughters-in-law to wish her dead, how could she imagine that I, her own flesh and blood, the daughter who was supposed to be the kind and considerate one, should wish her dead, and for such a selfish reason? Yet here I was, longing for her end.

It wasn't until we were on the train coming home that I managed to break the news that we'd probably find my mother at home. Franco started screaming and shouting at me and he went on and on until we were actually home and inside the front door. I could hardly make myself heard in order to greet my poor mother and my aunt, who were flabbergasted at this outburst. I asked how my mother was progressing. My aunt, after all her sleepless nights at her sister's bedside, was determined enough, once she got over her surprise, to say very clearly that my mother needed peace and quiet, that I was her daughter and so far I'd done nothing at all to help – all I'd done was to take my children on holiday, and now it was up to me to do my bit because the rest of the family were exhausted and needed a rest from it all. Franco gave in after this speech and apologised, and even offered his own bed to my mother. But she had already taken it anyway, since it happened to be the most suitable one for her in her present state.

My mother took full advantage of her situation. She had been at death's door and now she was gradually recovering her hold on life, so she ruled us with a rod of iron and insisted on absolute peace and quiet. I didn't know what to do with the two children, who created pandemonium in the next room until all hours of the night, laughing and bouncing on the beds. Their desire to cooperate seemed to have become a rare occurrence indeed. It was only at bedtime, with the lights out, that they ever gave me the feeling that they really wanted to help. My mother therefore suggested moving Marta into the study. This possibility had already been discussed and Franco too had agreed that Marta was growing up fast and would soon be entering puberty, so that it seemed only right to separate the sexes. I wasn't too sure about this and I felt reluctant to take such a step now, but I found I was alone in my view, and anyway I had to do something to provide the peace that my mother needed.

Marco's decline was instantaneous, and it almost caught me unawares as I tried to juggle running the house, nursing my mother and giving a bit more time to Marta, who – finding herself banished to the study and surrounded by its austere furnishings – had begun to have nightmares. I also saw signs that she was approaching her first period. Moreover I felt I had to make it up to her because the poor child had literally been ousted from the room that had always been hers. Her brother now barricaded himself in there as sole proprietor and refused to let her through the door. He flung all her treasures out at her, but kept for himself everything that had belonged to both of them, including all the hundreds of books and some of the toys, and he refused to allow anything to be taken away.

The atmosphere was pregnant with approaching trouble; we all moved around in it like characters in a play, unable to escape. My mother, who by this time was feeling better, retreated from the scene before the floodgates burst. One of my brothers came to fetch her by car and she left in torrential rain, which would have put most people off travelling, although any deluge must have seemed preferable to staying in our house. The departure of this outsider, who had both contributed to the heightened tension and yet in her own way had also been a steadying influence, left the four characters free to act out their tragedy. The chief actor now turned out to be Marco, whose tangled feelings had by this time formed a hangman's noose for him.

Now that he had a newly won territory of his own and because the outside world had become a place of untold terrors for him, Marco absolutely refused to let his sister into his room – or me either. When I forced my way in to clear up or do something for him, he would drive me out, kicking and shouting at me, and his father, instead of calming him down, actually encouraged him by yelling at me from which ever room he was in to leave the boy alone, as if I were trying to

28

kill the child. The only time that Marco left his room was when he went out for a walk with his father, but these walks were in the nature of an escape rather than something positive. Franco was in the same state as his son, full of feelings of rejection towards the female side of the family – and unconsciously he must have included his daughter now that she showed signs of becoming a woman. If we all went out together, it was not so much a walk along the street as a chase, because Marco was terrified of the soles of his sister's shoes and would do anything to avoid being behind her where he could see them. At home, when we were all together, Marco would avoid Marta as if she were a leper, saying that she smelt: his rejection of her was a really physical, instinctive thing. She had been the child closest to him for all the eight years of his life, and now he would have nothing to do with her.

No doubt one of the factors that led him to take this attitude was the hormonal storm going on in Marta's body, so that she really had changed her smell: she no longer smelt of milk, but of something indistinct and dark – not yet an adult woman's smell, but something that approached it. Marta of course suffered from this constant rejection by her brother. He had been her point of reference for years, and it gave her an appalling sense of frustration, so she turned to me for comfort, wanting my affection and unconditional love. And naturally I gave her my love, all the more readily because I could feel how soon she would be facing a new phase of her life. But this behaviour of mine was only further proof to Marco of my lack of love for him. And yet it wasn't true at all: no one will ever know what agonies I suffered at not being able to show him how much I loved him. But all my efforts in this direction met with the usual response. The only moment in the day when I managed to feel like an impartial and loving mother was when I served out the food, and in the end I was thwarted even in this. It began all of a sudden, and it took me quite a while to understand what it meant.

We were at the table. I had served out the food and we had started eating, when suddenly we realised that Marco was chewing and chewing on the same mouthful without swallowing it.

'What's the matter? Don't you like it?'

It was one of his favourite dishes. I always made what he liked in an attempt to reach his heart through his stomach, as they say. He didn't reply; he just sat there helplessly, chewing and chewing until a mess of masticated food began to run from the sides of his mouth.

'What are you doing? Swallow it down!' I said.

But his father, panicstricken, had rushed round to him: 'Spit it out! Spit it out!' he commanded.

This business of spitting it out was not something invented on the spur of the moment for the present emergency – it was a longstanding paternal order, repeated every time Franco suspected that a particular mouthful of food might hurt the children in some way. Recently he had only feared for Marco. Sometimes it was fish, and he was afraid of the bones, though I mashed each piece that I gave the children. Sometimes it was food that he thought might be off or in some way harmful – a most unlikely possibility, but Franco's anxiety made it seem realistic. Thus even the choice of a symptom has its own precise logic: since Franco was forever defending him against my so-called unfairness, Marco now saw his father as the only person who had his welfare at heart, so Franco's continual insinuations about the food were a message to Marco that any mouthful of food that his mother offered him was to be feared as a potential threat to his life. Marco had now internalised this suspicion and it had materialised as a real, tangible fear. A conflict had exploded inside his mouth between his survival instinct, which told him he was hungry and should eat up, and this fear, which was also an expression of his survival instinct but which told him to refuse the food as dangerous. But all this was happening at an unconscious level in the child, and we who were watching the performance were a million miles from understanding what was happening, so we couldn't offer the right kind of help – and certainly not quickly.

Caught between the orders from his two parents to spit it out and to swallow it down, Marco – after a struggle that seemed to last an eternity – chose the former course, and spat the food out. The pantomime began all over again with the next mouthful: he was too hungry not to eat, but his fear was stronger still. Marta watched him, half speechless, half laughing with amazement, while Franco and I sat there, unable to tear our eyes away from those slobbering lips.

This scene was repeated with every sort of food. He had a total block: all he could swallow was water and milk. We consulted our family doctor, the national health one who'd been so forthcoming over my own illness: he advised us to take the child to an ear, nose and throat specialist, and mentioned the name of the best-known man in town. We made an appointment and then waited an exhaustingly long time for our turn. The doctor did a very thorough and careful examination of the child and tested him with his equipment. Marco fought him off all the way through: by this time he was fast assuming the appearance of someone seriously ill. Franco was wide-eyed with terror and I looked my usual reserved self – my coldblooded reactions are notorious.

'Nothing at all! Absolutely nothing wrong! This child is perfectly healthy – at least in my opinion.' That meant in the opinion of someone examining this particular piece of anatomy with this particular physiology. We asked him what the cause was in that case, and he shrugged his shoulders. After some hard thinking, he advised us to get an X-ray of Marco's oesophagus and stomach done. Clutching at this piece of advice and at the starving child, we went off to look for a radiologist. The radiologist looked carefully at his oesophagus and assured us that there was nothing wrong there, no foreign body, no fishbone or pin or anything else stuck down there.

At this point we were in a real quandry about what to do next. I insisted that it was a psychological problem, but Franco is one of those people who don't believe in psychology – you can't touch it, you can't see it and it's more the province of charlatans than of science. However, we went back to our family doctor, who stuck out his bottom lip and raised his eyebrows in a most discouraging way because (of course, what could I expect?) he too belongs to the ranks of those who have no time for psychology and who consider it witch-doctor stuff.

Nevertheless, since he had nothing else to suggest, he allowed us to consult one of these charlatans. And it was then that Nestore stepped into our lives. He had married an old flame of Franco's, the girl-next-door from Franco's council tower block. She must have been attracted to that diffident and vulnerable young student who was so committed to educating himself out of the ghetto; he had addressed letters of fire to her – but only when lending his more refined pen to the adolescent longings of a bolder friend, who of course signed them himself. Old stories, buried in the past. Now, in this crisis, Franco contacted her to ask her for the loan of her husband's wisdom. We were invited round immediately: father and mother with their frightened and distrustful small child between them.

Nestore sat behind his desk, inscrutable and imperturbable, resting on his paunch like Buddha. He listened to the excited crossfire of Franco's story and mine and then said he wanted to talk to the child in private. Afterwards, he asked Marco to go upstairs and see their own toddler, and then he talked to us again.

'The child has a rather serious neurosis, maybe something worse than a neurosis. But it is clear that it has to do with you, it is the result of your conflicts. In other words, if you want the child to get over this, it's you who'll have to undergo the treatment.'

I said I agreed. I was already quite sure in my own mind that this crisis was connected with our conflicts. But Franco said he felt perfectly well, that he'd never been ill, and that the problem was to get the child to eat, otherwise he'd die. Nestore smiled a little bitterly. He must have realised straight away that he'd get no cooperation from this father. He prescribed some medicine, so as to give Franco the feeling that something practical had been done, and reassured him that the symptoms would soon disppear, but he also repeated that some therapy would be necessary, otherwise a different symptom would probably develop.

We left, I with some hope that we would hit on the right path, Franco sceptical and argumentative. He said he respected Nestore as an honest and intelligent person, but he couldn't see how he could help us with our problem, and that he had no intention of having therapy because he wasn't ill. I should go and get some treatment, he agreed, because I had all sorts of things wrong with me, and I was probably the root cause of everything – he'd always said it, and now it turned out to be true.

'I'm willing to admit that I'm partly responsible; but *why* have I got all sorts of things wrong with me? Don't you think you may have something to do with my getting ill? It seems obvious to me that there are things wrong with you too and I can't understand why you won't do something to help your own son.'

'I would give my life for my son. But I don't think this is the way to help him. When you don't believe in something, it's no good. I'll go straight away now and get this medicine.'

Marco took the medicine. But he continued to swallow nothing but milk and water. I used to add lots of sugar and a beaten egg to the milk, but solid food was no good – the block was still there. When our relations got wind of it, they came up with all sorts of suggestions; they were all quite sure that it was just lack of appetite. So Marco was sent off on pilgrimages to his grandparents and aunts and uncles. And wherever he went, the performance was the same: here is someone who is hungry, who is served exactly what he asks for and has no fishbones in this throat, yet what happens? He chews the first mouthful endlessly, dribbles it – all mashed up – from his mouth, makes a slimy mess all over the place and finally runs to spit it out. Our relations, poor things, did their very best and tried to get the child to explain. All Marco could say was that he was hungry but he couldn't swallow and he just had to spit it out. Did he maybe have a sore throat? No, nothing hurt him, but it was all closed up. Wasn't he afraid he'd die if he didn't eat? Yes, he was, but he didn't know what to do.

Our relations would bring him home, shrugging their shoulders helplessly. Franco and I were fading away along with Marco. I'd been back to see Nestore and begged him to help me. He had replied that it was I who had to help him: all he could tell me was that the child had spoken resentfully of his sister and had claimed I loved her more than I loved him.

Was I fair as a mother?

This question, put to me by the doctor, became, for me at

least, the key to the removal of the 'fishbone' that had got stuck in my son's throat. I had taken such great care to ensure that both children had an equal share of my love. I wanted them to have nothing to complain of on that score. I wanted them to grow up with a deep sense of fairness which they could bring to all their future relationships. That this very factor should be the cause of all Marco's trouble forced me to think back carefully over my relationship with him and with Marta, with whom he compared himself.

My second pregnancy had been far more relaxed than my first, because by then I had got over all the fears that you have the first time round. It was a natural birth, unlike my first experience when Marta had been wrenched out of me with forceps. The labour pains were not too lengthy or exhausting, I dilated normally and I remember, in the cold, clear sunlight of a March noon, feeling an irresistible urge to shit – not realising it was the baby pushing his way out. He was born with a strong, lusty wail, greeted by the cheers of the medical staff, who all chorused, 'It's a boy!' like a shout of victory. And the shout travelled quickly through the doors of the labour ward to all the waiting relations and then by phone to Franco. He was at home with Marta, who had tonsilitis, and when he heard the news he knelt down in the middle of the room and thanked God in his own way.

There were no problems over the baby's name – it all went off peaceably; when Marta was born there'd been an appalling uproar and a lot of resentment over her name. Marco's name was the same as my father-in-law's, and everyone – myself included – was pleased. I looked at my son hanging upside down in the midwife's hands, and he looked like a skinned rabbit. I looked at him tenderly and serenely, feeling that everything would be easy for him, all doors would open for him. Perhaps that's why I didn't have the moment of anxiety I'd felt when I'd first seen my daughter. I knew that she would have to push her way through life with nothing but her own strength to help her.

Just as with Marta's birth, I couldn't sleep the first night. The excitement of knowing that he was there in his cradle, separate from me, was too great. It seemed strange to think I'd no longer feel the kicking I'd felt inside me for the last four months. A great sense of peace and liberation descended on me and kept me wide awake and glowing. My heart ached for Marta, who had realised from the air of excitement the night before that I was going away without her. She had been so upset that she had become feverish and had got worse and worse all day, with a constant high temperature despite the prescribed penicillin. Franco said it seemed to be tonsilitis, but that even the doctor was mystified. I was sure that the temperature was really due to her pain at my departure. It was the first time I'd left her since she was born, one and half years before. The next day I put Marco to the breast and he sucked so hard – I'd never felt anything like it. The feeling of being drained of so much milk was almost a physical pleasure.

The few days in hospital passed quickly and I divided my time between enjoying this new child whom everyone admired and who was already beginning to fill out and look beautiful, and longing for Marta. By this time she'd got over the temperature but it was cold outside and she wasn't yet well enough to go out.

Still, I wasn't really worried about her, because my husband's parents were at our house looking after her. As a matter of fact, when they first arrived there'd been a big scene: my mother-in-law received the news that her youngest daughter had suddenly decided to get married and live in Milan, where the eldest daughter had already settled. My mother-in-law took this news worse than if she'd heard of her daughter's death. She collapsed, sobbing and screaming in desperation, much to the terror of her little grandaughter, whom everyone forgot in the drama of the moment. My homecoming was a red-letter day for me: I dressed the baby in his best little clothes and came home with him in my arms. The first thing I saw as I came through the door were Marta's two big black eyes, shining like live embers in her white, pinched little face. Her eyes searched for mine and then, bewildered, fell on the little creature I held in my arms. 'Look,' I said, 'here's your little brother who's come out of my tummy!'

I put the baby down on the bed, picked up Marta, and held her near to the baby so she could touch him. She smiled, but more as if she did it to please me than anything else. I had no particular problems with the baby. Our paediatrician had a look at him and pronounced him healthy, except for a slight tendency to umbilical hernia due to the umbilical cord not healing quickly enough.

But I did worry about Marta's behaviour. She forgot everything she'd learnt and regressed to babyhood, wetting herself again and refusing to feed herself. The worst times were when I fed the baby: I was almost always alone in the house and Marta couldn't walk properly yet. Anyway, Franco was so apprehensive that I didn't dare let her roam about the house while I was sitting feeding the baby. So I used to sit on a low divan and put Marta next to me with some toys. Then I'd take the baby on my lap and bend over to feed him. Of course my attention was then taken up with the baby. He sucked avidly, to his great pleasure and mine. There – wild kicking on my back! It was Marta expressing her misery at being neglected. At the sudden movement, the baby lost the nipple. His little mouth searched for it again after his sudden interruption of bliss. I put the nipple to his mouth again quickly, gently chiding Marta, but her response was more kicking, and each kick was harder than the last. In the end the baby broke into desperate wails. After a month of this, Marco began to refuse the breast when it was offered before anything could happen to stop him sucking. Because he didn't suck, I began to lose the milk, although I tried expressing it and taking pills to keep up the flow. I tried every trick I could think of to feed Marco when Marta couldn't see me, but it was too late. The doctor advised me to give up breast-feeding and give the baby bottles. I consoled myself with the thought that my milk had given him cradle cap anyway, and complied. It was this period of time I had to look at now, to try and find out exactly what had happened.

For example, when I realised how much it upset Marta to watch me feeding her baby brother, why hadn't I done something about it straight away? Even just for Marta's sake I ought to have done something. I should have remembered how upsetting her own experience of weaning had been. I had weaned her early because I had to go back to my teaching job after she was born and so she'd had to have

36

complementary bottles. My breast milk had decreased because I wasn't doing all the feeding, until I lost it altogether before she was four months old. But she had a very low tolerance for the artificial milk and suffered a lot of vomiting and diarrhoea, so in the end I had to put her on to solid food very early. That had worked and she'd begun to thrive.

I should have realised that for her to see me engaged in an activity from which she herself had benefited for such an extremely short time fully justified her reaction. I should have protected her from such an unsettling experience. And yet I carried on sitting her right next to me and forcing all three of us to go through what was obviously a traumatic process over and over again. Why did I do it? It's true that I was alone and that might explain it. It's true that the relationship between Franco and my mother was so strained that, although she lived in the flat below ours, we didn't feel we could visit each other much. There was also the fact that Franco was moody and difficult because he didn't like living in my home town. This was partly because of my family's financial disasters and their business affairs which – according to his standards of honesty – were shady, and partly because he considered the political ambience low-brow. He also suffered from his mother's constant recriminations on the subject of his absence from Bari.

So I tried not to burden Franco with anything else and I somehow felt it was more dignified to sort out my own problems over the children. I had internalised his opinion that it's the mother's job to take responsibility for the children. But despite this conviction, I ought to have told him about such a delicate matter as the feeding of the baby and Marta's reactions.

How come I didn't? The truth of the matter is that I obviously didn't focus properly on the need to sort out the problem. I must have borne the situation with a sense of fatalism, like something that can't be avoided and so just has to be lived through. Now why was that? I searched through my memory, amongst all the forgotten things that one throws in there like bundles of old rubbish into a dark attic, hoping never to see them again. Marco lay curled up in bed, visibly wasting away, his eyes bigger and darker each day, and suddenly I saw myself as a child, pretty much like Marta, maybe a little plumper. And I saw a scene very clearly, as if it were taking place before my very eyes, a scene I hadn't remembered in thirty-eight years.

I had been the happiest child in the world, a wanted child, welcomed into the world and loved not only by my father and mother but also by all my relations because I had been the first grandchild on both sides of the family. And although I was an early developer, my mother breast-fed me until I was eighteen months old. Society in her day still followed the old rural traditions, so I was still drinking her milk when I was toddling and chatting away and entertaining the whole family with my singing and dancing – a substitute for the television in those distant evenings.

Now, all of a sudden, my memory shows me, way back in the past, a picture of my mother leaning lovingly over a fat, rosy bundle of flesh, her white breast hard with milk, and me, standing rejected on the doorstep, sent off to my grandmother so I wouldn't be in the way with a brisk 'Go on, off you go, go down to Grandma's!' I went down to my Grandma, who was generous with her sweets and cakes, and I devoured them, filling myself with these love substitutes. It took me years to get over this compensation eating – it took the lean years of the war to do it. And after that brother, there was another and then another, so I never got my place back near my mother. She never seemed to care; she delegated the care of me to her own mother and my Grandma was delighted to oblige. She did her very best to take my mother's place in my heart, and she kept me tied to her apron strings in the shadow of her great, benevolent matriarchal figure.

That was how my infancy had been: unsuspecting happiness for all the first period, so that I drew from it great vitality and an optimistic faith in life, and then a sudden, cruel expulsion from paradise. And I didn't even find the small space in my real family that I ought to have had. I was sent away, in no uncertain terms, to seek what compensations I could find. Yet, however appreciable they were, they were always a painful second best. Not even the loving and

38

all-embracing relationship which I quickly established with my father could repay me for that loss of rights, even though my father became the centre of my universe until, on the eve of my adolescence when I was thirteen, death seized him from me.

But now I had an overriding need to examine this distant childhood trauma of mine and to try to untangle the noose from round Marco's neck. When I bent to feed Marco, Marta's kicking had triggered off a runaway process of identification with her. I had allowed her to do to me what I would have liked to do to my own mother when she sent me off so that she could feed my brother. And I had behaved exactly as I would have liked my mother to behave then – I had suffered Marta's reaction and let her reap the consequences. My whole being had longed for the punishment that my mother should have suffered. I had sat motionless beneath that kicking, masochistically enjoying the balm that finally soothed away the pain of that first wound that life had inflicted. There could be no other explanation for the way I'd allowed the situation to arise over and over again, to the point where I felt actual joy in it, the same joy that my mother had felt in offering her breast to Nino's powerful sucking – more intense sucking than mine had been. And in Marta, I had another me-child who spontaneously took my revenge for me, doing exactly what I would have done to my own mother if she hadn't taken steps to stop me by sending me off to Grandma.

So Marco had had to suffer at the hands of me-as-a-mother the revenge that I-as-a-sister wanted to take on Nino. But Marco as my son had suffered serious injury from this revenge, an injury that had never healed, no matter how much effort I had later put into recreating an equilibrium between the two children. I had tried to give them equal care, but perhaps I'd only given my daughter the treatment which belongs by right to the littlest child. I had indulged her spontaneous regression to her baby brother's stage instead of gently encouraging her to follow her own path forward.

What would be more just in the leader of a people which has conquered another people: to give everything to the former and leave the latter with nothing? Or to satisfy his own people to a lesser degree so as to leave some space for the conquered? Whatever he did, one of the groups would accuse him of injustice, but all things considered I think the second solution is fairer. It's not a very good comparison, but in that remote emergency I'd picked the second solution. I was trying to give Marco life, but at the same time I realised how much Marta felt cheated of her own hold on life, and so I tried to re-establish a balance by putting them both on the same level. I pushed one a little too fast and allowed the other to hang back – since that was obviously what she wanted to do. But now I discovered that this was a mistake and I understood why it was a mistake, and because it had been my decision, and mine alone, I felt guilty.

My sense of guilt was compounded by my next discovery: I had actually hated my mother and my brothers. I hated my mother in the same measure in which I had longed in vain to love her. I realised that all my later devotion and the spirit of self-sacrifice that I'd shown to her and my brothers after my father's death – when I'd tried to fill in as husband and father – had been nothing less than an unsuccessful attempt to compensate them for my hatred. I had found a way to make it up to them, so as to placate the unconscious resentment that I could not allow myself to feel. My moral conscience rejected my own bad feelings. Now I saw that my relationship with Franco, which I had cultivated against my mother's wishes, had grown out of that same resentment and that my old resentment had reappeared during my mother's illness, when I had longed for her death.

Later on I managed to go deeper into all this. However, at the time I am concerned with now, the overwhelming need was to find a way out of the situation we were all caught in. I had to find where it was that we'd taken the wrong turning so that I could recreate my relationship with my son. Marco could only swallow liquids, mostly milk, which he drank eagerly from a glass I held for him: so he'd regressed to those early months of babyhood when I breast-fed him and he drank blissfully, before the unexpected obstacle had arisen. I had stopped breast-feeding him to raise him to the same level as his sister, and he had unconsciously lived this as my refusal to give him life and strength. So now I had to retrace the path

40

through his psyche and reassure him that it wasn't true, that I *did* want him to live, with all my heart, and that I would do anything for him because he was my child, and the only thing that mattered to me.

The circumstances led me in the right direction: Marco was so weak from his liquid diet, inadequate as it was for an eight-year-old, that he caught bronchitis. We had been afraid that his illness might have nasty consequences, so he'd been taking antibiotics and this had lowered his resistance even further. Now he lay there in front of me looking quite ill. Suddenly I felt really frightened, actually frightened that he might die. I felt bad enough myself, exhausted from lack of sleep and food, and weak from my recurrent attacks – still treated as a heart condition – and one afternoon I suddenly reached the point where I just couldn't bear it any more. Losing my self-control, which perhaps Marco – like Franco – took for lack of love, I threw myself on Marco, sobbing desperately to him that I couldn't bear him to die, no, I couldn't live without him, that he had to eat, he had to, didn't he understand how much I loved him? Otherwise he wouldn't come through this, he'd die and I'd die with him because I'd no longer have anything to live for. And the child threw his arms round my neck, sobbing and begging me to help him, because he didn't want to die but he couldn't help himself, I had to help him, I had to . . . We lay there with our arms round each other, panting, then suddenly I let go of him and hurriedly went and got him a substantial meal – something pretty solid but which gave the impression of something liquid. I spoon-fed him, talking to him all the time about how our throats are specially designed to swallow food down the oesophagus without choking, because the air passages are automatically closed off, so he could swallow without any fear, nothing would happen to him, because his Mummy who loved him was there – and he must trust this love, he'd never lose it because he was my sweetheart, my pride, my own little boy.

Marco, now full of hope and confidence, watched my loving, tearstained face, and he ate and ate, without any difficulty at all. He ate it all up and asked for more, he jumped up and sat on the bed like someone suddenly restored to life, and ate a cheese sandwich and then a milk shake. Then he hugged me and I could hear our two hearts beating with a joy I can't express.

I was the only person who really saw what a miracle had occurred. All our relations merely commented that they'd known all along that the child would get his appetite back sooner or later. Franco didn't give me any particular credit for Marco's recovery, since he too was sure that the matter had resolved itself. And I claimed no credit for myself because I felt that any mother would have tried any, and everything just as I had done. I continued to feel that I was in Marco's debt: I thought it would be a long time before I'd really have made amends for the injury I'd caused him. As for Marta, she had taken such a loving and enthusiastic interest in her brother's rescue that she seemed to me the one real ally I could count on for the next step in the healing process. I explained to her what had happened as clearly and simply as I could, and she understood. So I asked her to help me, to bear with her brother if he was hostile towards her, and to be a bit more easy-going with him. I pointed out to her for the first time that she was the elder of the two, that she was growing up and becoming a woman and that it was right for her to create new areas of independence for herself instead of sharing her brother's world. She seemed to agree, and listened with rapt attention when I talked to her about the wonderful changes that would soon happen to her, how the hormones would mould her body and mind so that she would begin to look like a young woman. One evening as I helped her undress for a bath, I noticed with pleasure that you could already see the womanly body emerging: and she saw what I was thinking and threw her arms round my neck, pleased at my realisation.

I talked to Marco too, and told him the equally wonderful story about his own hormones and how they would soon make a good, strong young man of him, handsome and desirable. He'd already put on weight and there was no evidence of his recent fast. He was growing taller and his face was taking on a more adult look. Luciano, who'd been kept at bay during the bad times, was readmitted to the old games

42

and the talks about life – and things went back to normal. Back to normal meant back to the old atmosphere and back to the old power games. I didn't want that to happen and I tried to get Franco to take a good look at what we were all up to. I had an apprehensive feeling that we were in for more trouble. But Franco was as hard and impenetrable as one of those enormous sea turtles with their indestructible shells, and Nestore, to whom I occasionally went for advice, repeated his conviction that I would never get any help from my husband. And it was true that everything rolled off him and left him clean and unmarked, ready to make the same mistakes again.

I was more compliant and accommodating than usual because I still felt drained by the recent episode that had taken so much out of me and Marco. I tried hard not to provoke any irritable or hysterical reactions in the other members of the family. Meanwhile, encouraged and reassured by Marco's recovery, I continued to sift through my past and to investigate Franco's. Now that I was aware what a lot of restrictions and inhibitions surrounded our lives, and how much of that tangled mess still needed unravelling, I wanted to work out what exactly had lead Franco and I to choose each other in spite of all the difficulties. What was the basis for this union of ours which seemed proof against all the storms and onslaughts? Our relationship had weathered them all, and we were still obstinately in love with each other.

I tried to reconstruct Franco's infancy from a multitude of small clues, from things he'd told me and episodes I'd heard from his mother and brothers and sisters. I tried to knit it all together and tell him the story as it seemed most likely to have happened. He listened and took it all in, but he did so in that detached way of someone listening to a story that has nothing to do with them. He hadn't worked it out for himself so it was not a stimulus for real growth or deeper understanding.

Franco had been born into a more complicated family situation than mine. His parents were probably more ill-matched than mine were. His father came from Liguria in the north and his youth had been wild and adventurous. He'd been away from home from the age of fourteen and he'd been everything from a waiter to a test pilot, and had run through every imaginable erotic experience, without anyone to stop him. Franco's mother was a young country woman from Puglia in the south. She had a very high-spirited and emotional personality, but no outlet for it in the narrow, oppressive society she lived in. Her father loved her but she had a step-mother who tormented her and was jealous of her. Her own mother had died in giving birth to her and she grew up with the aching void of that missed comfort, that life-giving first love that can never be replaced. Franco grew up in this strict working-class family, the third child after a sister and a brother, closely followed by two more brothers and a sister. His father was the stern ruler of the household and the upholder of moral law. His mother was a childish person who never accepted her role as mother and indeed saw her children as her own future protectors. She brought them up to be her security for her old age and Franco was caught between the older children, who claimed their seniority rights, and the little ones, who needed care and attention. Thus he learned to do without much attention himself. He grew up timid, hypersensitive and lacking in confidence, always ready to obey instantly if only he could get a little love and attention in return. He was the helpful one of the family, the one who used to do all the queuing at fountains and food shops in wartime, the one who gave his bread rations to his hungry little brothers. He was forever trying to think of ways to please his mother: he'd buy her a banana or some other special treat just so she'd be grateful and give him a smile. He was a good pupil; he never missed a day at school, never failed to do his homework, never played up in class. He was the one who feared his father's punishments most, yet he was constantly and savagely punished, often enough for something one of his brothers had done. He was the one who heroically repressed all his desires, sublimating them in his studies and his self-sacrificing helpfulness, and never ever indulging in that sin of sins, masturbation. He had suffered very violent repression on that score and the memory of it was lost far back in his infancy.

When he reached early adolescence his elder brother died of a cerebral haemorrhage after a motorbike accident and his elder sister fled to Milan, so then he had to act as big brother as well as his mother's comforter. She was under so much strain from her husband's reign of terror and his constant sexual demands that her mental equilibrium had suffered – especially after the loss of her two eldest children – and by now she really was in need of love and care. Franco gladly took on the task of looking after his mother: at long last he had found a role which gave him a sense of self-respect and which made him feel enough of a man to approach the other sex. These first contacts were all bought for cash and undertaken with the utmost caution. This is more or less how Franco was when I first met him. That's why he seemed to me like a virgin forest, waiting to be discovered and explored, a mass of wonderful, unexpressed potentialities which I found fascinating and irresistible.

My life experience to date had been quite different, but I was emerging from a period which had been just as dormant and troubled for me. I had spent the preceding years with my grandparents, who had taken possession of me in my early infancy. My relationship with my mother and brothers was always an incomplete one. The only life-giving relationship I'd had was with my father, but he died just at the wrong moment for me, just as I was about to enter the golden years of adolescence. That brought me up short – I'd been obliged to act as a substitute for my father after his death. I had taken on the responsibility of helping my mother and trying to control my wild brothers. I made this sacrifice willingly enough because I wanted my mother's love and, indeed, for the first time she noticed my existence and she did finally make me feel loved and wanted – however cynical her behaviour may have been. My sex life had not got past the masturbation stage. I lived through this phase with a frustrating sense of guilt and occasional resolutions to sublimate my desires, not into my schoolwork but into something creative, because I did have a certain amount of versatility and imagination. Every so often I'd fall in love with someone, but the austere rules of my grandparents' house forced me to limit myself to platonic expressions of love. When I met Franco I was still just like an adolescent with hardly any sexual experience. Thus we came together from very different backgrounds and we lived through the sensations of first love that should have happened years before. We wanted somehow to retrieve those lost years which we had both spent fulfilling family responsibilities and starting our teaching careers – we'd jumped in at the deep end and were teaching at secondary school by the time we met.

What I really wanted to get to the bottom of now was not so much the man/woman aspect of our relationship – maybe I wasn't ready to look at that yet – but Franco's role as a father and his collusion in my role as a mother. Why was it that Franco, right from the first wail of his first child, had been so exaggeratedly anxious over the children, and why had he become even more so with his son? With his first child he'd behaved almost normally, and when he'd sometimes gone too far I'd put it down to his extremely emotional nature and his lack of experience. It had even been something I found endearing, so warm and easy and affectionate had been his relationship with his little daughter. It often reminded me of the relationship my father had always had with me. It was with his son that things had started to go really wrong and his behaviour had become pathological. It was then that he'd begun to check and double-check to see if I'd carried out my childcare duties perfectly. It was then that he'd begun to take such a morbid interest in every last detail of the child's life, and to threaten me with all sorts of reprisals, no matter what I did in the interests of my son's health, as if I were out to harm or kill him. His accusations all dated from the same period and, however hard I'd tried to be a caring and loving mother, he'd always hammer home his message that I was a bad mother. Why had he done that? Surely Franco couldn't have had the intuition to see in me then what I had only just worked out now about my past and my motivations? Franco, who was so blind to the workings of the human psyche? Or could he? Sometimes I was tempted to believe it. But common sense told me that this wasn't a plausible explanation for his behaviour, because I'd been so quick to adopt my 'fair-shares' style of mothering. He wouldn't have had a leg to stand on.

It seemed more pertinent to take a close look at the interesting relationship he'd had with his own mother. That's where the key to it all must lie. It didn't take much to see that Franco had started identifying with his son, reliving in Marco his own childhood drama of maternal neglect. His mother had a big family to care for, with several children younger than Franco, not much money, and a strict, demanding husband to deal with. And she was an unstable and immature person, unable to give herself unstintingly to her children or to feel any sense of fulfilment in her role. She herself had been in constant need of love, care and encouragement.

Now Franco was reliving in his small son all the precariousness of his own early life, which had been all the more frustrating and insecure because of his domineering father who, instead of offering reassurance, had terrorised his children with his heavy-handed violence. For example, I had noticed that Franco felt sick and dizzy if he looked down from a balcony, and this phenomenon was connected with two recurrent childhood experiences. He himself had told me about these episodes in casual conversation, without attaching any significance to them. One was the experience of being left for hours on the balcony by his busy mother when he was little. He'd often end up asleep with his head against the railings until a neighbour came round to remind his mother that the poor child was still curled up out there and that it went to her heart to see him like that. His mother had confirmed this story, but she only told me to show what a good, quiet child he'd been, so unlike his noisy, demanding brothers. Then there was the story of how his father used to pick his sons up and throw them in the air and catch them, for fun. Years later, his father told me how all the other boys loved it and yelled for joy but Franco was so frightened that he used to shut his eyes and scream in terror. That, said his father, just showed that he had no guts, he wasn't like his father – and thus didn't deserve so much of his father's respect.

It was clear to me from stories of this sort that Franco hadn't been treated as a sensitive child should have been. He'd been humiliated by these experiences, and these feelings of mortification had conditioned his adult life and made him anxious and insecure and liable to get extremely upset at the least little thing. This attitude of anxious watchfulness had been the theme throughout Marco's babyhood and it seemed to me that this must have been one of the factors in the child's crisis. Marco had been persuaded to live his relationship with me in a state of anxious fear, as if my love were a prize that might be snatched away at any moment. This had given him such a sense of frustration and deep rooted insecurity that it had turned into a real persecution complex. The pattern of violence that Franco had encouraged in Marco must in the short term have satisfied Franco's unconscious thirst for revenge on his sacred, untouchable parents. But what this violence actually produced was a defensive reaction on my part, and this is what Marco saw as my lack of love for him. This chain reaction could have gone on for ever, had I not broken it with that decisive act of love.

But it was difficult to work within this new awareness without any cooperation whatsoever from Franco. He thought all this reflection on the past was little more than the ravings of a sick mind. Once he'd got over the fright at Marco's refusal to eat, which the whole family had now classed as lack of appetite (a reassuring diagnosis with no threatening overtones), Franco carried on where he'd left off. His attitude to the children and to me was the same as ever, and it was no use my asking for his help or trying to make him see how important it was to understand what had happened.

I was on my own, and even my appeal to the children to try to achieve a more wholesome lifestyle for themselves went unheeded. And no wonder, since the mechanism we were caught up in was too complex for any one of us to escape from it alone: unless we worked together, we'd never get rid of it. Our days had become even lonelier than before. My mother would have liked to come and visit us every so often, but we discouraged her, saying we needed to be alone to sort ourselves out. We hardly ever saw any of Franco's family for the same reason. We stopped seeing friends and acquaintances, so none of us had any contact with the outside world except through school – Franco and I as staff, and the children as pupils. That was our sole social outlet.

But life at school was also frustrating and traumatic, because that mind-paralysing institution acted as a sort of bulwark against anything new, against any sign of a different way of life or more creative ways of thinking. And despite all our contradictions, we were trying to do something new. Thus the relationship that each of us had with our respective school communities was certainly not a liberating one. We brought to that relationship all our own unresolved problems and then we found the relationship itself tense and controversial since the people at our schools rejected our ideas and we rejected the schools' rigid, habit-bound structure.

At lunchtime Franco and I would engage in what amounted to a competition to see who was the more progressive teacher, and the two children couldn't help but compare our ideas with those of their own teachers. What they chiefly picked up on was the controversial attitude we assumed, and this inevitably led them to look critically at their teachers and propose alternative methods. This was seen as insubordination and the teachers retaliated with reproofs or with disciplinary measures, or by handing out lower marks than the children deserved. Because school was the only real reference point outside the family, the relationships formed there became loaded with the same heavy tension that characterised our interaction at home. This didn't help the children's attitude to their schoolwork. As it was, they rejected the methodical and factual way in which the school subjects were taught, and did their best to take a more personal and critical view of their studies that would lead to a more creative choice of jobs. If schools were different, these ideas might have been more favourably received but, as it was, their attitude created constant problems, especially for me, since one of my tasks was to make sure that the children did their homework and came up to standard. But I will talk about this further on.

At the moment I want to recall another event that occurred at that time and which had an unsettling effect on my relationship with Franco. His elder sister, after various attempts to move back south near her family, had finally found a way to return to her native city. Everyone was filled with new hope for the future: Franco himself, and all his brothers and sisters, saw this return to the tribe as an opportunity to unload some of their responsibility for their parents on to Teresa. Their mother, with her constant demands for comfort and moral support, was forever stirring up marital crises amongst her children by her criticism of their partners and their child-rearing methods. My father-in-law was always dragged into these dramas and forced to side with one member of the family or another. He too felt more hopeful and went about whistling light-heartedly. Franco's mother was in seventh heaven. She was sure now of her daughter's moral support and loving care in her old age. And Teresa herself was pleased at her success and had persuaded herself that this long-awaited move back to her place of birth would turn out to be a good thing for her and her children.

By now I'd reached a stage in my analysis of the family ties that bound these people together – and now bound me too – which prevented me from sharing this universal hopefulness. After my initial euphoria I soon realised that these hopes were doomed to disappointment.

What had led Teresa to give up the solid economic position she'd worked so hard to achieve? Over the last few years she had deliberately left it all behind to move south and now she was moving right down to Bari. This was the question I asked myself and I tried to reconstruct her story, using what I knew of it and trying to fit the bits together in spite of the areas of doubt and darkness.

Teresa was born at a time when her mother was still a simple, naive country girl. She even lacked the combination of homely wisdom and passive resistance which mothers traditionally pass on to their daughters: only her own mother, whom she'd never known, could have initiated her into the dark mysteries of motherhood. Thus the poor girl, at her first pregnancy, watched her belly grow enormous and asked her neighbours how the baby would get out. When these good women realised the extent of her ignorance they couldn't bring themselves to enlighten her about her body, and anyway they thought she'd soon find out by herself. She was not aware of any special hole. Intercourse with her husband was a traumatic experience for her and she suffered it as a violence to be fought off. So when an older woman who'd had several children revealed to her that the baby would come out of her knee, the unconvincing explanation left her bewildered but silenced.

After she'd given birth, and suffered all the dramatic and unexpected violence with which she was treated, this woman found herself with a little creature in her arms, facing a maternal role for which no one had ever prepared her. She hadn't even the unconscious, distant memory of mothering that most women can call upon and which passes for maternal instinct, despite the fact that human nuturing has to be learnt like everything else. Her other babies appeared one after the other and so her eldest daughter was put to work around the house at a very early age, learning all the domestic duties of a proper little housewife. Teresa was an intelligent and sensitive child, and she learned everything she was taught with great speed and skill. She was so willing and so good at her work that she soon became an extremely valuable help. It is easy to imagine what her motivation was. It must have been a hard life, but she earned her mother's love and gratitude, and these were rare treasures because her mother was constantly busy at her many tasks – all of which she suffered as impositions.

It wasn't long before Teresa's compensatory behaviour forced her into making a heavy sacrifice: as soon as she could read and write she had to leave school. That was the end of her education. She was such a clever, creative child that her teacher begged her mother to let her continue at school. But there was no escaping her mother's requirements: the decision to withdraw her from school was taken in the face of Teresa's helpless tears and protestations. It left an indelible mark on her soul, and from then on she saw herself as a victim gradually being bled to death by the needs of her younger brothers and sisters. Nevertheless, she had to put a brave face on it so as to retain the grace and favour of her torturers: at least they could be grateful to her while they abused and violated her spirit.

Her mother did give her ample credit for her increasingly

competent efforts in the role of assistant housewife. Although she thought the sacrifice she'd asked of her eldest daughter was necessary and unexceptional, she was aware that it was a sacrifice. Time-honoured tradition dictated that the daughters should stay at home and serve the sons so that the sons might have what they required – a place in the world beyond the domestic walls. However, the mother wanted her poor daughter to have some way of earning her living in the uncertain years to come, so she sent her to dressmaking school. Teresa became an expert and skilful dressmaker. It goes without saying that all her early efforts were used to clothe the big, growing family.

Teresa was growing up and was turning into an attractive, shapely girl. When she began to emerge as a sexually mature young woman, she was eager to marry and take the one step that was open to her: promotion to slave in her own family. At least then she'd have a boy who loved her and saw her as the centre of his domestic life. But her father refused all her suitors: none of them seemed good enough to him. She had plenty of young men after her who were ready to show serious intentions in order to win her, but her father thought none of them worthy of the honour of her hand. It began to look as though he was guided less by considerations of his daughter's happiness than by his own jealous possessiveness. He needed to keep the family maid, the one person who was a help and a comfort to his wife, since the latter was less and less able to cope alone with the heavy burden of the family.

In the end Teresa ran away from home with someone. The reparatory marriage could not be organised because she had no dowry, so the only solution was to send her off to the north of Italy – to the more liberal-minded atmosphere of Milan – to look for work or, better still, marriage. Her brother went with her: he too was looking for work to finance his university studies.

Teresa met her ideal man: Geremia was from a peasant family in central Italy. He too had come to Milan to search for work and he had found a job at the Pirelli factory. He was really in love with Teresa, and he was the sort of straightforward and open young man who sees a woman in terms of a wife for himself and a mother for his future children. They managed to get Teresa's father to consent – he felt obliged to save the family honour – and Teresa settled in Milan. Her brother returned home, chiefly to try and calm his parents down and help his mother face her husband's rage. The father accused the mother of giving her daughter the wrong sort of advice and of encouraging Teresa to leave home to escape from his authority.

This same elder brother was going through a troubled and unsettled period. He was torn between the need to be supportive to his mother and the need to pay for his own university studies since he couldn't expect anything from his father. These were the post-war years, and the financial state of the family was precarious. The boy was also active in socialist politics and he put a great deal of creative energy into this area. Then, one cold, wet day around Christmas, he fell off a friend's motorbike and died. He'd been released from the hospital emergency department, where the doctor on call had failed to diagnose the brain haemorrhage that killed him. When Teresa heard of his death, several months later, she went through a very bad time indeed. By then she was worn out by her own fight to save the life of her baby daughter, born prematurely at seven months. The baby was in an incubator for weeks before she could survive by herself, and even then she was weak.

Teresa's mother, summoned by her daughter's desperate tears and by feelings of guilt, went up to Milan to see her as soon as she could. It was past her understanding how a young woman could fight so hard, so persistently, to save the life of such a little scrap of a baby. The child seemed to turn away from life, refusing food and vomiting anything she'd been patiently persuaded to take. Teresa's mother had never had to struggle like that: all her children had grasped at life with a strong instinct for survival. All she'd experienced was their greedy sucking, which had drained her very life blood so that she'd almost had to defend herself against them.

Now she had to watch the great strength and determination that her daughter displayed and perhaps, unconsciously, she felt that here was the motherly love that she had missed, that she had never received nor been able to give. She felt acutely jealous of the little baby who now seemed to be stealing her daughter's heart for ever, depriving her of Teresa's love which had always felt more like a mother's than a daughter's. Teresa, for her part, had a vague conviction that she'd been cheated of her mother's love, that she'd been forced to earn it by hard work and self-sacrifice. She seemed to draw new strength from her enormous battle to keep her baby daughter alive. It was as if she enjoyed being able to show her mother how much one can feel for a daughter if the love is there. Then her mother had to go back to her own family, who needed her, and she left feeling unhappy, frustrated and shaken by the experience in Milan. The two women took up antagonistic·positions and this rift ran through their ensuing correspondence, so that for the next few years their letters to each other were a crossfire of accusations. The mother complained of being cruelly and thoughtlessly abandoned, while the daughter complained of her mother's lack of love and care for her – and they both bemoaned the misery and pain they felt.

Teresa's attitude to her family became increasingly critical and hostile. The more emancipated and advanced view of society that prevailed in Milan contributed to this process. In the north, women were beginning to acquire a more equal and respected place in the outside world, and Teresa's desire for revenge on her family gave her the strength to show them that she was no fool and that even with her modest dressmaking qualifications she could earn a good living. She developed such a degree of skill and creativity in her work that she was soon in a position to set up a dressmaking business of her own and employ other workers. Her clothes reached haute couture standards, her signature on the label became well known, and her clientele was drawn from the cream of Milanese society. She gradually acquired an air of refinement from her constant contact with the elegant élite of Milan, whom she dressed in those years of the great economic boom. This aura of style put her a cut above the rest of the family, and when she came south to visit once a year in the heat of summer, she delighted in showing off her ladylike manners, her well dressed children, Liliana and Sergio, who'd been brought up like rich children, and the solid financial position she'd attained. The only false note now was her working-class husband, Geremia, whose worn, lean appearance put one more in mind of the long hours he'd sweated at the assembly line than of the health-farm slenderness of the leisured classes.

Teresa's mother was proud of this transformation and regarded it as a personal triumph. She was unable to see that everything her daughter had achieved was entirely due to Teresa's own courage in defying her family and taking her life into her own hands, thus radically changing her seemingly inevitable destiny. And so her mother began to shift her criticism to a different tack. She pointed out that if only Teresa had had the patience to wait, she would have been one of Milan's most eligible women, now that she had such a brilliant business position and could offer such a large dowry. She could have made a much better marriage. As it was, she had a workman for a husband and had to live hundreds of miles from her mother, who could have helped her in her work and given her so much valuable advice. And there she was, alone, with a house to run, a business to supervise and two demanding, spoilt children who seemed to need a dozen servants and an endless stream of money.

Teresa was still quite an ingenuous person at heart, and she didn't know how to reply to her mother's confident and logical line of reasoning. Her mother knew her weak spots, because basically Teresa still felt an outsider in Milan, rootless and insecure. She often boasted that her brothers down south were all graduates with good jobs and warned Liliana and Sergio to say that their father worked in an office if anyone asked them. Moreover, she was certainly lonely, in spite of all the classy people she knew. She must have missed the company of her relations, especially now that all her brothers and sisters had families of their own, which made the family relationships richer and more varied. Yet fate had decreed that she should be the one to live away from home, away from the warmth of family affection and familiar ways and, worst of all, away from her mother's love. Probably she also felt she still owed her mother some care and affection.

Geremia was worn out by his work and, although he loved her very much, he couldn't give her the sort of attention she felt she needed. Liliana and Sergio did nothing but make demands, and their demands were endless. They asked for everything that children nowadays – brought up in a consumer society – feel they have a right to expect. They were growing up pampered and choosy, with classy manners and complicated food habits. They had difficulties adapting to their environment because, although they'd been born in the north and were familiar with the way of life, they could never feel quite as much at home as their peers, whose families had lived in Milan for generations. Teresa was proud of them, but the effort of raising her children to middle-class standards made for a lot of tension and fatigue in her life. One of the reasons for her overwhelming desire to see her children firmly established in the middle class was the thought that all her brothers and sisters had risen above their working-class origins. They were all professional people now, climbing the social ladder at whatever cost to themselves.

The society emerging in those years took as its model the world of the very rich. And the rich had abandoned their old standards of honesty and reliability and they now thrashed their way forward by fair means or foul, creating the new morality of the rat race. We were all to see the consequences of this way of life before too long. Teresa now began to suffer psychosomatic headaches and gastric upsets, and she became increasingly vulnerable to her mother's complaints because they revived all her old guilt feelings. Her physical symptoms offered a new subject of attack for her mother, who pointed out that Teresa would be better off living near her family. She declared that children are no help to their parents, and only the affection of a mother and brothers and sisters can support a woman in her middle years. Furthermore, said her mother, after such betrayal and abandonment as Teresa's, it was only right and proper that she should come home and give her mother some loving care now she was getting old and had so many ominous aches and pains.

And so Teresa began to move south by stages. There were all sorts of applications for a job transfer for Geremia, any amount of string-pulling on the part of her brothers – especially Franco, because his socialist party was now in power and he had therefore gained a certain amount of credit and importance in the eyes of his family. The first stage of her move was Rome. The family found it hard to integrate there, especially the children, who were now at secondary school. With their rather reticent mentality, they looked down their noses at the Roman vulgarity displayed by the triumphant rulers of the world – which is how the young citizens of the capital city saw themselves. Teresa had to give up her flourishing business and go back to making clothes at home for a well known boutique and for a few select clients – hard enough to find now that off-the-peg clothing was coming in. Teresa faced all these difficulties with great courage, going against her children's wishes in the matter even though they complained bitterly. Her only reward was that she felt a little nearer her mother. And, all the time, she was on the lookout for a way to take the next step in her descent towards the south.

The next step didn't look so easy, partly perhaps because Teresa was aware that she couldn't expect her children to follow her further south willingly. Or perhaps she enjoyed living in Rome, where she was near her in-laws' patch of land and could help herself to their fruit and vegetables. Anyway, she persuaded her mother to move there, recounting to her the delights of the eternal spring weather and cheap, plentiful markets of Rome. Her parents moved to Rome, but their stay was short-lived. It was difficult for them to adjust at their time of life, hard to move away from everything and everyone they knew, including their other children, who had at least made the old people's lives more interesting. The move also coincided with the protest years when all the kids were out on the streets demonstrating, and the two grandchildren were enthusiastic in their political commitment and took an active part in what was going on. So the generation gap yawned and there was mutual intolerance and violent quarrelling. The young people rejected their grandparents and the old people retreated, horrified and beaten. They were angry with their daughter and felt that she'd spoilt her children and given in to them until she was completely under their thumb and deprived of her dignity and parental authority. Once again the letters between mother and daughter became acrimonious, but this time Teresa was less able to defend herself because she too was terrified that her children would get into trouble or fall victims to their own protest. There were plenty of victims amongst those bold, proud kids in those years. She was soon begging Franco to pull some more strings and get Geremia's job transferred further south. And she had plenty of support from her mother, who divided her time between pressing Franco to do something quickly and urging Teresa to prepare for the move south.

I was called on as well in that emergency: they asked me to persuade a casual literary acquaintance of mine to help Teresa, and I did so, pleased to be able to do my mother-in-law a favour. This was before Marco's neurosis had opened my eyes to all the games. My mother-in-law was full of gratitude and assured me over and over again that it would be a wonderful thing for me to have such a clever, capable sister-in-law living nearby. But for the time being we were caught up in Marco's drama and we could no longer watch what was going on in the extended family. By the time Teresa made her triumphant entry into her native city, I was not so blind to the power games and thus I was unable to share the rest of the family's joy.

As soon as my own private nightmare receded I looked at the situation in Franco's family with new eyes. And to me it looked bad, on all counts, for Teresa and her family. Now that she was back in the bosom of her family, Teresa seemed to have surrendered at one blow everything she'd striven so hard to achieve in her years of rebellion and independence. She no longer had an income from her work, and it seemed difficult to earn anything by dressmaking, even within the large family. Her sisters seemed unwilling to recognise her experience and expertise as a dressmaker and hung back. It was only on the odd occasion that I was persuaded to make use of her services, because I wasn't one for thinking much about clothes anyway. So Teresa's family had to make do with Geremia's wages, and the rising cost of living, plus the high rent for accommodation, ate into the purchasing power of their small income. Their two children had got their diplomas and left school: now they were looking for jobs at a time when work for the well qualified was getting scarce.

They had to rely on their relations to help them find work. Teresa's brothers knew a lot of people and were certainly well placed to find jobs for the two kids, and this they undertook to do – especially Franco – but time went by and the jobs did not materialise. So Teresa found herself in a position of inferiority, which she masked to a certain extent by drawing on the savings from the fat years. Meanwhile she spent her days running to her mother's house, because her mother – determined that Teresa should make up for her twenty years' absence – acted fragile and helpless. Teresa also struggled to keep abreast of her children's demands: they were angry and hostile over this second move south. For various reasons, it had happened at a bad time for them. There was a decline in the protest movement and a spreading sense of political apathy, especially in the south of Italy, and this got Liliana and Sergio down. They also felt the lack of any social contacts that might have helped them to integrate into southern society, since they had already left school and had not yet found work. Thus they had no friends in the south, and felt isolated in a family whose efforts were entirely focused on maintaining its hard-won middle-class status.

Teresa and her family might have found an ally in our family – at least we were engaged in an open, on-going attempt to pinpoint the problems and solve them – but unfortunately it was just at that time that we'd shut ourselves off from the rest of the world. We couldn't come out of our huddle because Franco hated the idea of any outside influence. He wanted to keep his family at arm's length because of the conflicts developing there and he was particularly anxious not to be drawn into taking sides with his sister: that would have brought down his mother's wrath on his head and Franco regarded her displeasure as the worst thing that could happen to him.

It was a very difficult period. Teresa knew how ill at ease her husband and especially her children were, and she felt guilty about it. She took out her feelings on her mother and brothers – they had promised so much help in finding work for her children and yet, now that she had moved south, they took their time over the search and left Teresa to deal with her children's growing resentment. Teresa also felt that her brothers and sisters had pushed her back into her old role of family dogsbody. They seemed vastly relieved to hand her all the responsibility now that she was back at her mother's side, with the old pattern re-established.

Her mother absolutely refused to listen to the complaints that she heard from her daughter and grandchildren. In her view the kids were selfish, lazy idlers, lying on their beds all day long instead of helping Teresa – who was busy running after her mother and arguing with her. She thought Geremia was common and not good enough to be a member of their family, and that Teresa had allowed herself to become a slave to her husband and children, losing all her self-respect and her love for her family of origin – which was anyway a more respectable and prestigious family.

That was enough to shatter the initial illusions and start all the old arguments off again. The whole family would take part in these quarrels whenever they met at their mother's house – or at her bedside when she took to her bed for want of a better attention-seeking ploy. Of course, it was a complex and difficult situation and it probably did make her feel ill. Anyway, she used her illnesses as an excuse to accuse one and all: they had selfishly deprived her of the love and moral support which would have made everything bearable and might have given her back some peace of mind. I watched from the sidelines and I was very sorry that Franco was generating so much bad feeling in our own family because I would have liked to help Teresa somehow.

I did explain to her what we'd been through and I told her that in my view she ought to save her energy to help her children. They were still having a bad time trying to get some foothold on the work front and battling with their feelings of being outsiders in the extended family and in society at large. They were both introverted and fragile kids, full of uncertainties about their lives. Teresa didn't understand what I was trying to say – perhaps she couldn't understand because I was talking about the very mother—daughter relationship which had been the painful knot around which her own life had developed – or maybe it's more correct to say it was the knot that had enveloped her life. Perhaps she was still blind to the significance of recent events. At any rate, Teresa expected her homecoming to be a real reward for all her years of exile. She expected to be treated like the prodigal son, welcomed and fêted, and was still waiting for all these good things to happen, convinced as she was that the celebrations were only delayed because her self-centred brothers and sisters couldn't come to terms with their moral debt towards her. Had they forgotten how much she'd done for them when they were little? My talk with Teresa elicited only her resentment and the resentment of my mother-in-law, who heard what I'd said and took it as an act of defiance against her. Franco was of course angry with me because he'd instructed me to keep out of it. He thought I wanted to exacerbate the tension between mother and daughter, either out of pure spite or because I was a witch who saw evil even where there was nothing but good. But I didn't feel any ill-will towards my mother-in-law; I understood why she behaved as she did. She was a victim of a situation over which she had no control, and I felt sorry for her. However, I couldn't condone her behaviour when I saw its effects on her children and grandchildren. I thought they had a right to live their own lives, especially the younger members of the family, and that it was important to ensure that the youngsters had the mental space they needed.

I felt pretty much the same about my own mother at that time: I saw the same self-centred attitude in her and, although I knew she had a right to live her life, I felt she ought not to hamper her children's lives. Now that I deliberately kept her at bay, she used to go to my brother Federico's home more often. She stayed there for increasingly long periods of time and there she was in constant close contact with her daughter-in-law and two grandchildren. I had news of an atmosphere of mutual awkwardness with frequent quarrels and violent scenes. These all arose over the most trivial matters, but the basic cause was always the same: my mother interfered in their lives, she invaded their space, and then took their defensiveness as a personal offence – and an offence to her institutional role. I tried to warn my brother of this as well. I pointed out what it might do to his domestic peace. But he too reproached me – and so did my mother when she heard what I'd said. They both condemned my thinking as onesided: I thought too much about my own children and not enough about my duties as a daughter. This I couldn't deny, but it seemed to me that the patriarchal structure of society was crumbling and we were now left with a society composed of nuclear families – just parents and children. This new structure didn't function well yet and it needed a lot of rethinking. I couldn't yet see how to change it or how to make it work but I thought that, as long as there are small children around, the duty of mothers and fathers is to look after them and not to worry about their own parents. If this was humiliating for the old people, then let them stop interfering as if it were a right of theirs. Let them forego this continual handing out of old-fashioned advice. Their outlook had been forged in an older type of society and had little to offer the new order. It was up to them to create new spaces for themselves and leave their children to sort out their own lives, especially since it was now the latter who were in the midst of life's battles.

Both sides of the family objected to these views of mine, for different reasons. Everyone found a sympathetic ear in Franco, and the counter-fire coming at me was nerve-wracking. I felt exhausted and frustrated by it, and this didn't help to keep an even keel with the children. The two children had their own reasons for their feelings of hostility towards me and I tried hard to understand what they were.

I had an uneasy feeling that something terrible was about to happen, something so dangerous that I didn't know if I'd come through it alive, and yet I didn't know what that thing was, and I started begging everyone for help and support. And everyone looked at me as if I'd gone mad, as if I were raving. Then I felt really powerless, as if I could do nothing by myself, and the more I tried to escape from the quicksand, the further I got sucked down. When the danger is visible, everyone can see it and then at least one knows exactly what one is fighting, and help is easier to come by. But I was the only one to apprehend the threat, and all I could do was wait – with my ears and eyes open and my heart thumping. Nevertheless, I still had to get on with my daily life, trying not to show the fear that was gnawing at me.

It was Marta who worried me now. When Marco had been ill I had turned to her for help and understanding. But once over his crisis, Marco's feelings towards his sister were as hostile as ever. He drew strength from his father, who watched over him more anxiously than ever and wanted everyone to treat his son like a little god. Marco broke off all relations with Marta and refused to have her in his room. She was excluded from all his games – now he played wilder and more exciting games with his friend Luciano, who was a frequent visitor. The suppers I used to make for the three of them before Marco's illness were never resumed, because nowadays we all dined together when Franco came home. Marta spent her afternoons alone in her room. It was a cosier place now because we had moved the old study furniture into the living room and bought more suitable, colourful furnishings for Marta.

The girl seemed to be waiting for something. A few months previously she'd had her first period and at the time she didn't seem at all upset by it. She took it quite naturally, and was full of pleasure at her new state. I had prepared her for this event with great care, remembering my own traumatic first period. My mother, alerted by the cleaning woman, had suddenly seized me and shut herself up with me in the bathroom. There she thrust a huge bundle between my legs and pushed me out again without uttering a single word. I had lived through the next few days tortured with guilt, hiding from my father and brothers and secreting the evidence of my bloody crime under the wardrobe, even though I knew I'd inevitably be found out and have to listen to unspeakable insults from my angry mother. That's why I'd done my best to shield Marta from an experience of this sort and had tried to communicate to her that menstruation is one of the most wonderful things that happens to us women. In this state of grace, we announced the event to the male side of the family. Franco was troubled but he was quick to put his arms gently round Marta and congratulate her. Marco was openly jealous, as if he felt pained that he had not attained any equivalent male experience yet.

But this important event should have been hailed with

some recognition of adulthood. And that didn't happen – what happened was quite the reverse. Marta had already had a foretaste of fatherly repression a few years before. It was when the first Barbie dolls appeared on the market. Marta wanted one and I bought it for her. When Franco came home that evening, Marta showed him her beautiful new doll, wanting him to admire it. She was shattered by his response: he went mad, screaming that I was a bad, immoral mother and ordering her to throw that 'pornographic' doll away at once. And yet all that was wrong with the doll was that it had a woman's body with hips and breasts – the genitals of course were formless, as they always are in dolls.

Marta burst into tears and refused to throw her new doll away. I leapt to her defence, and shouted at Franco that he was a mean heartless father – something out of the ark, a fool, a paranoid nutter and so on and so on. I was so determined not to give in on this, not to be beaten, that in the end we won and Franco shut up about it. I tried to wipe the memory of this awful scene from Marta's mind by making and buying lots of dresses for Barbie. But Marta didn't play with the doll for very long; it soon ended up amongst the pile of forgotten toys. I didn't see it again; my mind was on other matters and I forgot all about it.

After that episode I began to notice that Marta was less at ease with her father than she'd been before. She was still fond of him, she liked his sense of humour and admired his political activities and the ideas he propounded, but something had changed. Franco, with the proud possessiveness of a father watching his daughter grow in grace and beauty, would sometimes pull Marta to him and give her a big hug – but nowadays she pushed him away and seemed irritated and embarrassed by it. I pointed this out to him and said maybe he should have a little more respect for her new sense of reserve. Nevertheless, I found her attitude hard to understand because my own relationship with my father had been very demonstrative right up to the time of his death.

Now that I was watching a father—daughter relationship I began to think back to my own experience and explore it. My father had really loved me, and I really loved him. It was he who had made me feel like a person and who defended me against my mother's demands. She would have liked to make a household slave of me, but he defended my right to knowledge and self-expression and encouraged my interest in the arts. When I wasn't at my grandparents' house, my mother expected me to help with the housework, but my father – deaf to her reproaches – would take me off on walks or along to the library where he was head librarian. Through him I had the opportunity of meeting interesting, thoughtful people, and I grew to love the world of ideas. The people I met thought me a sensitive, intelligent girl, full of potential, and they treated me as such. I certainly owe it to my father if I was able, at first, to choose a satisfying life. His views on women were not particularly enlightened, but he loved me and he had confidence in my abilities. Thus I was able to lead a life I enjoyed instead of submitting to the sort of upbringing that most girls got in those days. When he died I was still young and I found myself up against a hostile and uncomprehending world.

Later on, when I reflected on the part my father played in my life, his stature diminished somewhat. Amongst his letters, which I found after his death, there was one to my mother, written during the catastrophic bombardments of Foggia by the Allies, when everyone was evacuated and people feared for their homes and property. He was writing to keep her spirits up and one of the things he said was that he was sure the whole family would one day be reunited in the family home and that he imagined me in the beautiful drawing room, as a radiant bride in white standing next to the man I loved. He used to talk to me sometimes about this dream of his, and about the grandchildren I would bear him – though he didn't think he'd live to see them. So in fact my father couldn't actually envisage any other future for me but the usual one of wife and mother. I'm sure he hoped I'd be happy in my marriage, although his own miserable experience of matrimony might have made him think twice. His sexuality had been limited by illness and he had looked outside his marriage for affection, sublimating his desires and seeking intellectual and so-called spiritual satisfaction elsewhere.

If his view of my future was so unexceptional, why had he

taken the trouble to encourage my intellectual gifts? Why had he bothered to save me from my mother's attempts to initiate me into the art of housewifery? She had protested loudly enough and threatened him – and me – with all sorts of reprisals. Maybe other factors had played their part? Perhaps the very circumstances of my early life that I had found so frustrating and hard to bear? During the long years of my infancy, when my mother had sent me away from the family so she could concentrate on her sons, what had my father ever done to keep me near to him? He had accepted my absence passively and unprotestingly and had seemed quite happy just to see me on my rare visits home. It's true that the intensity of our feelings during these visits led to a very strong emotional attachment between us. I felt a lot of resentment towards my mother but somehow I didn't hold my father responsible for my painful state of exile; I turned to him with an open heart and found that I could express myself with him in ways that were impossible with other people.

So living with my grandmother had been a decisive factor in my life. She was busy with her own family and particularly with her younger son, the future Paul Getty figure. She also had a demanding, bad-tempered husband to deal with, and her role as the boss's wife to fulfil. The workmen used to come to her for first aid or restorative drinks when they got hurt on the job, and on festive occasions she would be on hand with plentiful refreshments and a benevolent smile for the workers' new fiancées or newborn babies: her smile was the seal of the master's approval. All these duties left my grandmother very little time to see to me and so, although she certainly had no unusual ideas on the subject of my future, by default I led a pretty free life, without any specific conditioning.

Thus I managed to grow up 'wild' and undomesticated and I was prone to rebel if anyone tried to curb me. My absence from home saved me from the restrictions that would have been my lot if my mother had kept me at her side. I would have been trained from girlhood to do all the jobs that make the eldest daughter into a vice-mother, like Teresa. Why did my mother pass up this opportunity? It would have been easy for her to buy my cooperation with a few smiles and kind words. Maybe *she* wanted to rescue me from the usual fate of women? That destiny certainly weighed heavily on her: she herself had had an exuberant and potentially wild nature and she had been obliged to suffocate her natural tendencies. Her illusory reward was motherhood, and she had greeted each new pregnancy with joy despite her premonition of new chains. When I grew up and accused my mother of not having loved me, this rescue operation was her oft-repeated justification.

For a long time I refused to believe her, because she herself had sought ways to curb me. But now I believe her. I believe her because, in those early years when the mother really identifies with the daughter, she did unconsciously save me from the destiny that she herself had suffered. She had suffered that fate because she had held on to her mother's apron strings, so she did the only thing she could have done to save me at a time when there was no consciousness in society of a woman's right to be a person: she sent me away from her.

The fact of the matter is that when someone close to us behaves in an unconventional way towards us, we find it hard to see it as something positive. I realise now why Marta was unable to give me any credit for the efforts I made on her behalf in a period of my own awakening consciousness – I would almost call it a period of mere presentiment. The first steps I took to decondition my behaviour were so unsure and so heavily criticised on all sides that Marta herself saw them as bad mothering and all my efforts counted against me. And I felt so inadequate that I couldn't even justify my behaviour, and so I tended to accept her view of me.

Now, when had my father become aware of me as a person? It was when I reached puberty: I had grown up wild, with plenty of space and freedom, and at that age I was ready to establish an unexpectedly rich and vital dialogue with him, so that we became essential to each other. That is why he chose me as the privileged companion of his walks and his afternoons at the library. His visits there were taken up not so much with routine work as with various meetings with interesting friends and colleagues and intelligent, cultured women, with all of whom it was possible to have satisfying and free-ranging discussions. Any and every philosophical or political opinion – even anti-fascist and anti-clerical views – could be expressed there in complete freedom, and this was the basis of my future growth and consciousness.

This allowed me to glimpse the 'male' world, and I liked the look of it so much that I wanted to stay in it. I hadn't yet realised that those pastures were forbidden to my sex. When my father died, my access to that world disappeared and I was left with a great sense of loss. But I am using hindsight now. At the time I'm speaking of, when I was right at the beginning of my consciousness-raising process despite years of personal reflection, what I wanted to recall was the emotional side of my relationship with my father. Whatever other elements of respect and intellectual admiration were involved, where did my delight in him lie? I enjoyed his physical presence, and although he himself was so reticent that I can't remember a single caress, he obviously enjoyed me putting my arms round him, stroking and kissing him and sitting in his lap hugging him. He never rejected the spontaneous affection I showed him, and it was I who slowly became less demonstrative, mostly because as I grew more like an adult woman, he was wasting away. His illness made him look increasingly fragile and vulnerable, until it was he who needed help and protection. And I hastened to offer my help whenever the occasion arose.

I felt as if I wanted to hold him safe in my arms all the time, and it hurt me that I couldn't. This was partly because of his condition, but also – although I was not conscious of this – because of the powerful incest taboo which must have been behind his own constant reticence and which I gradually began to feel too. In the last few months of his life he suffered a stroke, and became no more than a body, suffering and yet unaware of its own condition. He was as helpless as a newborn baby and I helped my mother to nurse him day and night. Some of the inhibitions which had made up that wall of reserve between us disappeared then, because all I saw of my cultured, intelligent father was a body that resembled him. Now he was nothing more than a living body with elementary needs, grimly hanging on to life and completely self-centred in his indifference to our fatigue. Day and night – but especially during those stifling summer nights when the hot wind blew from the south – my ears were full of his wild-animal cries for help. I'd run from my burning hot bed with nothing but a flimsy dressing gown on, and bend over his suffering face. Then I felt a ferocious pleasure in showing him my young, naked body. I didn't care that what little I had on my top half fell open; I revelled in my provocation. He was defenceless and all he could do was to turn his agonised eyes away. This dreamlike episode soon disappeared from my memories of my dead father: naturally I remembered all the positive things about him, creating a figure upon which I strove to model myself.

The amazement and turmoil I felt when this fragmentary scene from the past came back to me, plus the sight of Marta and Franco's present relationship, must have allowed something inside me to rise to the surface, because one night shortly after this I had a dream. I remembered it when I woke up, the way one does sometimes if it is a significant dream. I dreamed I found Franco making love with Marta and in my dream I felt as if I were suffocating with jealousy. Then I reflected that my mother must have felt jealous of the tender demonstrations of affection I had showered on my father, just as she had felt acutely jealous of the intellectual women that my father frequented, those women who had appreciated his cultured, intelligent, witty personality. I thought too that before I had established my communicative relationship with my father, I must have been jealous of my mother when I saw them looking, if not affectionate, then at least intimate together.

So then I realised that Marta must feel the same way about me when she saw Franco and me kissing and holding each other – as we did often enough, even if two minutes later she saw as at each other's throat again. In point of fact I had noticed that Franco went in for this sort of exhibitionism far more often than usual. I call it exhibitionism because there was no parallel improvement in our sex life and I had wondered if he were doing it to excite Marta's interest: and indeed, that did stir up all the feelings I'd dreamt I had, as well as a feeling of rivalry. In fact, I reacted by making an effort to regain my legimate place in Franco's heart. And I succeeded: I had made at least a rudimentary attempt to release my repressed sexuality and to express a greater range of erotic feeling in my relations with him.

This revealing dream discharged my fleeting jealousy of Marta. At the same time it made me realise how urgently my daughter needed some space of her own. The narrow confines which had so far contained her wonderful vitality were fast becoming a straitjacket. Marco had some compensation for his unsatisfying experiences in the outside world: he had Luciano's friendship and company. But Marta didn't even have that – the afternoons of fun and games with her brother were well and truly over. Perhaps part of the trouble was that she couldn't even talk to Luciano any more. He was just a shadow disappearing into her brother's room, and that was one more humiliation to bear. I no longer went for walks in the park or in the pine grove with the children – that had been an outlet for Marta's energy and an opportunity for her to talk. She had no real best friends: she had gradually lost touch with her infant school friend and she was cut off from the girls she met at her junior school by all the restrictions that her father imposed on her. In the morning it was he who marched her to and from school, like a bodyguard, and in the afternoon it was he who always refused point blank to let Marta accept any invitations to go out for a walk or to a birthday party. Yet these are the only opportunities for girls of that age to communicate with their peers. When they are in a group it gives them the strength and courage to exchange those words and looks that are the bases for their first social interaction. That's where their first love affairs blossom, with little notes and brief encounters. At least, that's how it works in our sexually repressed southern Italian society, and it hasn't changed much in the last few years as far as that particular age group is concerned.

At school the sexes were rigidly segregated. Marta never had any opportunity to meet the boys, unless briefly and at a distance, because they went into school and came out at different times; the gym and the toilets were separate – even school trips were one-sex-at-a-time affairs. For various reasons she was the odd one out in her class as well: she was more than a year younger than her classmates, her father was a teacher at the same school, and she also had a very different background. This background was a curious mixture: she had less personal experience of the outside world and yet she had the unconventional ideas and tastes that she had picked up from her contradictory home life.

I realise now that I didn't do anything like enough to loosen the vice that was tightening on her. Although I saw what was happening, all I did was to warn Franco over and over again that no good would come of it if he carried on in his authoritarian way. And, of course, whenever something happened to increase the usual level of tension, I used to quarrel with him. And the cause of these quarrels was always the same: his absolute inflexibility. He justified his behaviour by holding forth at length on the dangerous society in which we lived. He described to Marta in the most apocalyptic terms all the traps that awaited a young, inexperienced, well-developed girl like her at every street corner of the city. And to back up these warnings he used to tell us the gory details of every single crime that was committed anywhere in the world, implying that all this wickedness was concentrated in the few square yards around our house. To convince himself of this he took to buying scandal mags, over which he pored with morbid interest. He did try to make it up to Marta and to Marco, whom he wished to keep off the streets for other reasons – by showering them with books, records and gifts of all kinds, and by keeping them stocked up with enormous piles of stationery. He hoped that these mounds of paper, pencils, rubbers and so on would keep them at their desks from dawn till dusk.

Marta seemed content to lead this sort of life. She never complained or protested about her father's orders. Indeed, she used to say that she didn't want to go out, and she refused all invitations. Both she and Marco spent their time painting or drawing. And Franco would point this out to me to show me how wrong I was to worry about her and argue with him. He said the girl had none of the feelings I attributed to her, that she was still young and as long as she didn't want to lead a different sort of life it was silly to go putting ideas into her head. We ought to be glad we hadn't got one of those daughters who give their parents more trouble than the sons.

His reasoning left me unconvinced. But once again, I found myself alone. It seemed that I saw things that no one else around me could see, and all I could do was keep my anxiety to myself. However, Marta was not as happy as she wished to appear. Her behaviour at school was proof of this: she was forever breaking rules and getting into trouble. The teachers were constantly complaining about her to her father. They complained as gently as possible, saying they didn't want to offend a colleague, but really, such appalling behaviour was intolerable . . . And they would hint that, considering what sort of ideas he had, it was hardly surprising that his daughter, being younger and more naive, thought she could fight the whole institution.

This hurt Franco very much because throughout his school career, both as a pupil and a teacher, his attitude to the institutional rules had always been one of strict observance: as a pupil, he'd needed his qualifications and, as a teacher, he valued his job! So he took these complaints very hard, apologised for his daughter, and then home he'd come, bursting with rage, and let fly at Marta over the midday meal. He addressed his words to me as well because he claimed that I encouraged her. I had to stand by my principles – which were actually the same as those Franco professed – and I said yes, I did think Marta was in the right. I said I thought the way in which she staged her protests was rather extreme and liable to have the opposite effect, but that didn't invalidate her ideas. I did not believe, as Franco did, that one should only speak from a position of power, but I did think that the protest would be more effective if it were more carefully worded: discussion rather than antagonism seemed a better way to fight the battles. I went and talked to the headmaster and with the various teachers, and I even asked for a special meeting of the class council to be convened – unthinkable in those days, before parents had any formal say in how schools were run.* I'm sure the only

* In Italy class councils were composed only of teachers until 1974, when legislation was passed to allow the participation of a certain number of parents as well.

reason they agreed to this was that Franco and I were both teachers and he was on their staff. During the meeting I said that frankly I thought the reason for the girl's behaviour was that the school fulfilled none of her real needs, and that the things she demanded were the very same things that the junior school reform bill proposed to offer. Thus it was the school which failed to come up to the pupils' expectations and if a particular child was aware of this problem and showed it, the teachers ought to examine their consciences before pointing an accusing finger. It was pretty amazing that they let me say all this, but they soon came back at me: theirs was the best school in the area, any defects were due to organisational problems, and anyway, if the girl took such a precocious and unnatural interest in such problems, it was our fault. We should have encouraged quite different activities; politics are best left in the hands of the authorities and the democratically elected politicians, whose duty it is to deal with such matters. It was the old story – keep politics out of the home and off the campus! I said that I completely disagreed. Nevertheless, I had to recognise the fact that we as parents were at fault in not allowing the girl to mix freely with her peers and develop other interests which were certainly just as important to her personal growth.

Franco and I began to quarrel again about the children's lifestyle. But all I got this time was a chorus of dissent, because now Marta took sides against me too. She said I talked a load of bullshit, and proudly claimed sole credit for her battles with the school authorities. Shortly after all this there were local elections and Franco was one of the candidates for the socialist party. So we suddenly found ourselves in the midst of the political battle. Marta plunged enthusiastically into helping her father with his electioneering. We all helped, hoping to show that it was still possible for an honest socialist to get elected in spite of the crowds of power-seekers. But when we advised Franco against joining forces with someone who just wanted to use his reputation for integrity, he ignored us and entered the alliance. It was his downfall – he lost the election.

He lost a lot more than the election: he lost Marta's

respect. She had admired him for his principles and his integrity. Now she accused him of being a coward, of being servile and insignificant. Maybe I was wrong not to defend Franco on that occasion, but I wanted the truth more than I wanted domestic harmony. Franco said I encouraged Marta's negative feelings and I denied this. I tried in vain to get Franco to look critically at his own behaviour: it seemed to me that someone who can admit their own mistakes is easier to admire – and love – than someone who's always right, no matter what. It was no use. Marco, out of a sense of male solidarity rather than conviction, took his father's part and once more the family split down the middle.

Just before we went off on holiday, something happened to add to our state of tension and confusion. It took place in Teresa's family. She had recently come to see that my warnings were not so far out and perhaps the advice about her children would have been worth following. By now things were escalating out of her control and she was just a helpless victim of events. Her son Sergio, after months of hanging around waiting for a job in Bari, had taken off with a backpack for England. There he'd met a girl from the north of Italy and they had gone back to her home town together. He found a job in a paint factory so as to earn a living, although he wasn't used to that sort of job and the toxic work environment made him ill several times. However, in the meantime he took a state examination for elementary school teachers and got a permanent job in an infant school, abandoning his university plans now that a degree seemed superfluous. Teresa implored her brothers to find her son a job in Bari, in the hope of having him home again, but it was too late: Sergio had married his girlfriend so that their imminent baby would have a proper family.

Teresa was dreadfully upset at this sudden departure of her affectionate, intelligent son, and so she failed to notice that her daughter Liliana was struggling with far more serious problems. Liliana had lost the companionship of her beloved brother and she felt very alone. She had a boring temporary job, no friends, no relations she felt close to, and a desperate need for some warmth in her life. In this mood, she'd got together with the first person who'd come along, and now she was pregnant. The bomb exploded when the boyfriend absolutely refused to marry her: at that point her parents and all her relations set about persuading her to have an abortion and save the family honour. Liliana refused: she wanted the baby at all costs. Indeed it seemed to have become her main aim in life. The whole tribe abandoned itself to endless quarrelling and fighting. It was the subject of every family meeting. Those who had belonged to the 'right to life' camp suddenly upheld abortion and declared they would never permit a bastard to be born into their family. Those who had always believed in the woman's right to decide, and who had hitherto been regarded as promoters of abortion – as if abortion were some sort of pleasure – now became anti-abortionists, and sprang to Liliana's defence. Liliana was determined to have her baby, even if it meant being labelled an unmarried mother for the rest of her life.

Naturally, we belonged to the second group. We tried to point out to Liliana that an abortion would make life easier for her, but we stopped as soon as we realised how very determined she was. We agreed with Teresa that Liliana obviously saw her baby as a saving grace in a life full of disappointed hopes. And whereas that might not be the ideal approach to motherhood, it was her own life she was saving, and no one was offering her anything better. So we tried to get the rest of the family to accept and respect Liliana's decision. The first to capitulate was her father, Geremia, and gradually all the other members of the family gave in, though of course they were not uniformly convinced or kindly disposed.

Marta had followed this whole episode with great interest, and had displayed so much warm human sympathy and solidarity with her cousin that everyone had been surprised by her mature attitude and the clear thinking she had brought to the various family discussions.

We set off on holiday feeling shattered, our minds full of thoughts about Liliana's future. Marco was gradually growing out of his asthma, but it still seemed a good idea to go and take the curative waters once in a while, and so we were bound once more for the spa.

That year we spent our holiday in a little village in Romagna, but there was something very wrong – with all of us – and it was smouldering just below the surface. The children couldn't find anyone to make friends with, so Marco hung round his father and Marta hung round me. The tension between the two of them was so bad that, instead of putting the children in one room, we each slept with a child. I had a recurring nightmare and its atmosphere hovered around me. I didn't talk about it with anyone and I tried not to think about it, but night after night my sleep was filled with horrible visions. They were always about Marta. I saw her running through dark ravines, or fading like a ghost into the recesses of a mysterious old house. I saw her being swallowed up in a stormy sea under a leaden sky and I couldn't reach her – couldn't save her. I felt that she didn't want me to rescue her, even if she was going to die. I'd wake up with a start, sweating and trembling, and I'd look to see if Marta was still alive and lying next to me. It almost surprised me to find her sleeping quietly.

A few days later Marta had an unusually painful period. She didn't feel like leaving her room or coming down to lunch. Nevertheless, we had a tray of bland food taken up to her room, and we tried to persuade her to eat. Actually we were more worried about the waste of a good meal, for which we'd have to pay anyway, than about Marta's feelings. Marta did eat, but then she burst into furious tears, shouting at me that I was cruel and didn't understand her.

We didn't have many days of our holiday left. After this scene I noticed that Marta ate cautiously, almost as if she were afraid the food might hurt her. Apart from this she seemed quite calm. We left Romagna and went down south to Gargano, where we'd rented a house by the sea for a month. We spent most of our days on the beach, in and out of the water, and Marta often asked me to go for long walks with her. I could see that she wanted to talk and that she wanted to confide in me. But she didn't know how to begin and whenever I tried to help her, she drew back, frightened, and started talking about everyday things again. In the evenings we used to go and walk through the village, mingling with the crowds of foreign tourists who were just beginning to discover that wild, unspoilt part of Italy. Then we'd go to bed and, while Franco and I spent some good, healing time with each other after our recent separate nights, the children – who had a room together this time – played and fantasised just as they used to do when they were small. They seemed miraculously to be friends again, even if it was just for that hour before bedtime.

But after a while Marta started feeling ill again. She would eat her meals with a good appetite, enjoying the fresh food and delicious country bread, but afterwards she would start crying because her stomach hurt her. I tried her with soothing herb tea, I kept her on bland food for a while, I checked if she were constipated, but nothing seemed to make any difference: the minute she finished eating, she'd start crying and crying. She couldn't understand it herself. After a while she'd calm down and then she was perfectly all right again. She never seemed ill at any other time of day. Franco and I were really puzzled and each time we hoped it would be the last and prayed that the strange pattern would disappear. But it didn't, and Marta began to be afraid of eating. She began to refuse certain foods and she ate smaller and smaller amounts. But the quality and quantity of the food didn't seem to make any difference to the way she reacted, and the aftermath of eating became steadily more violent. Then my mother arrived – she had arranged to join us on holiday – and she busied herself cooking special dishes that she was sure would stimulate Marta's poor appetite.

By now the phenomenon did look like a failing appetite because Marta sat down to the table so reluctantly and picked so miserably at her food. But I knew that her appetite hadn't changed – it was her fear of the consequences that made her act like that. She was afraid of that mysterious enemy inside her that turned everything she ate to lead. Indeed, Marta did eat her grandmother's delicacies – they were too delicious to resist. But afterwards she sobbed more desperately and uncontrollably than ever. Nothing could comfort her: she rolled around her bed in agony and it looked as if some unbearable weight were crushing her. Each time it lasted for longer. And as long as the fit of crying and pain lasted, all words of comfort or support – or even reproach – that Franco and I and her grandmother could muster had one and the same affect: they just made Marta angrier. She would scream at us, and you couldn't tell if she was screaming for help or screaming to be left alone.

A local doctor came and had a look at her. He said it was nothing serious; maybe the sea air had made her irritable. He advised us to leave her alone and said it would clear up of its own accord. I remembered an episode from Marta's childhood. I first took her to the seaside when Marco was only a few months old. Marta had suddenly stopped eating on that occasion as well. She refused her baby food and it upset me very much to see her looking so peaky. I had called a local doctor and he told me to ignore it, assuring me that the child would ask for food herself in the end. And she did. Although I felt terrible serving our meals and pretending to forget hers, by day two she gave in and came to the table, dipped some bread in the tomato salad and ate it, and then ate the tomatoes too.

After that she never refused to eat. But it made me realise that she preferred to eat our sort of food and that she wanted to eat with us. When we went back to town, she seemed to enjoy the baby food I made for her little brother and she swopped back again. I understood then that she saw food as a social affair, and she didn't want to eat by herself. Now we tried to do the same as far as we could. To avoid making her feel out of it we put the food in serving dishes in the centre of the table and everyone helped themselves to whatever they wanted. She took more than anyone else, as if she saw it as a challenge. But the result was just the same as before; if anything, her anger grew wilder and fiercer than ever.

We'd spend the rest of the day discussing the problem. We spoke in hushed tones, so as not to be overheard. I began to feel more and more upset with my mother because, while I was becoming aware that the phenomenon was something really serious, she maintained that Marta was just spoilt and that this business of screaming her head off over nothing should stop. We ought to cut out all the sympathy and leave her to scream until she got tired of it. Franco looked increasingly harassed and bewildered. He felt unable to make any decisions and clung to me, begging me to figure out what was the matter with the girl and try to help her. Then the sun disappeared and it started raining, and it rained ceaselessly until the house seemed dark and damp. My mother seized this excuse to leave, and I didn't try to prevent her from going because her presence did nothing to help me keep my sanity.

Once we were alone the situation seemed to close in on us again. It poured with rain every day. Even if the sun came out occasionally, we'd just about make it down to the beach before the clouds reappeared, and we'd get caught in the downpour as we fled home. Back inside the house, time dragged interminably, and through the low windows we could see the dark waves swelling under the heavy, threatening clouds. The view reminded me of the scene in my nightmare and suddenly the ominous warning of that dream seemed very real, very close. I would have liked to go home, back to the city. But we told ourselves that the weather might improve and make everything look more hopeful. And it seemed a shame to waste the rented house. The children too were torn between the desire to stay and the temptation to leave early, and thus the days went by, all identical.

Marta ate less and less, and each day her screaming lasted longer. She screamed abuse at us now, accusing us of wanting to destroy her, wanting to kill her. She reproached her father for making her go to his shitty school, and me for not stopping him. She warned Marco against going to the same school, especially the section where Franco taught:

'Save yourself!' she shouted. 'At least you can save yourself. Refuse to go, don't let them trap you! Poor you! You'll have Dad as a teacher, they'll make your life a worse hell than it is already! Save yourself, Marco, listen to me before it's too late!'

Marco didn't say a word. But he was getting more and more upset, and one evening he couldn't stand the screaming any more and he suddenly broke down and had hysterics. Franco and I were at our wits' end. Franco however, remained stolidly unapproachable. He refused to listen to any criticism and he refused to rethink any of his opinions on the children's upbringing. As far as his school was concerned, he objected that plenty of his colleagues had children at the school without this being a drama for them or for the kids. It was just his bad luck, he claimed, that he had awkward, difficult children – and worse still, an uncooperative wife who'd undermined his fatherly authority and thus done the children no end of harm.

'I envy my friends,' he proclaimed. 'They all married humble, submissive women who work and who brought a home to the marriage. And they've got good, obedient children who don't create all these problems.'

I didn't take much notice because I was trying to work out what was happening to Marta, but I couldn't help reminding him how often I'd warned him that his handling of the children was wrong, and now here were the consequences. We certainly hadn't realised the gravity of the problem yet because Franco merely replied;

'Consequences! This is nothing but an upset stomach or some fool thing like that! Their grandmother is right – these kids are so spoilt they make a huge fuss over the least little thing.'

We were frightened and upset, but at night we tried to forget it all and we spent hours in each other's arms, like two survivors surrounded by the wreck of their ship. It was Marta's birthday at the end of August and we'd always celebrated this event with a special meal, and cakes and ice creams. Marta was worried:

'How will I manage to eat all that stuff? You are going to make it, aren't you?'

I saw that she wanted me to make all the usual party food, and I thought maybe it would cheer her up and help her get her confidence back. If we didn't celebrate her birthday it would look as if we'd given her up for lost.

I made a deal with her: 'The day before, you can eat as little as you like – only a tiny bit if you want to. Then on your birthday you'll be able to eat more without any problem.'

She agreed it was a good idea, and that's what she did. The day before she hardly touched anything at all and in the meantime I prepared a picnic lunch to eat on the beach.

A pale sun came out on the morning of her birthday, but there was a cold wind blowing and Franco didn't fancy going down to the beach. Nor did Marco, who always avoided anything uncomfortable or out of the ordinary. But I begged them not to disappoint Marta, so at lunchtime we duly filed down to the grey, deserted beach. The wind was raising little eddies of sand. It certainly wasn't the relaxed party atmosphere I had envisaged: Marco sat shivering under the beach umbrella which he was using as a windbreak and Franco told me to get a move on and hand out the food. It all seemed forced and artificial. Marta sat cross-legged on the sand out of the shelter of the umbrella and faced the wind bravely. She bit into her sandwich hungrily, as if she expected it to turn out all right this time. Marco ate miserably. Franco and I ate standing up, like two ridiculous puppets, not knowing what to say or do. The food tasted bitter to us. We even took photos. It was the tradition at birthday parties.

Then all of a sudden, a horse bolted. It escaped from its owner and galloped crazily along the beach. We all turned and fled, and in the fear and excitement of the moment Marta forgot to have her usual screaming fit. But that was the last proper meal she ate.

When we went home, each day seemed like another knock on the head: the same obsessive ritual over and over again. Each time Marta ate a smaller portion of food and each time the scene she made afterwards was more dramatic. Her screams echoed through the apartment building, which was filling up again with people returning from their holidays. Our family doctor came to see what the trouble was, but Marta refused to be examined. He said it was just an adolescent phase, and advised us to encourage her to be more active, to get out and about and take an interest in other things, because he thought we didn't give our children much freedom. He was right, but what could we do about it now? Marta wouldn't even go out. She hid in her room like a wounded animal and snarled at us if we spoke to her. She spent a lot of time drawing. Sometimes she'd come out and talk to me, and strangely enough she was looking forward to the new school term. This would be her last year in the junior school and she said this year she'd really make a revolution, she'd fight to get the teachers to change their attitude. I talked to her about the syllabus for the third year of junior school and told her how interesting and stimulating it was, and she seemed glad at the idea of getting back to her schoolwork.

She had lost the last of her puppy fat and she looked taller and slimmer: her schoolfriends and her teachers thought she suddenly looked more beautiful. But she was eating less and less and in the end she stopped eating anything but fruit. And finally the last little piece of apple – her only food – finished up splattered on the wall. Marta didn't mean it to hit the wall – she was aiming at Franco. After that she didn't eat any more and a few days later she stopped drinking even water.

Of course, we did everything we could think of. For a start, we used every form of persuasion with Marta because, however much we tried not to make a drama out of what was happening, it *was* dramatic. We begged and threatened to try and convince her to eat at least enough to keep herself alive. And the entire extended family crowded round to offer their advice and opinions. So did the few friends in whom we'd been brave enough to confide. But the phenomenon was so strange, so weird and unbelievable, that hardly anyone would take it seriously, and we felt that people thought we were making it all up. We became reticent and rather defensive: we seemed to be living in a dimension far removed from everyday reality.

We went to the experts. We consulted doctors and psychiatrists. They gave us unhelpful advice of a very general nature and told us to bring the girl for an examination. But Marta was adamant: she had turned her back on us and on the whole outside world, determined to hang on to the bitter end without accepting any help from anyone. She wouldn't even accept a glass of water – that old standby in times of trouble. She had cut herself off from everything, building a shell around herself that nobody could penetrate. She went to school each morning and sat at her desk, a little thinner each day. When she did talk it was only on an intellectual, objective level – both in or outside classes. She seemed out of touch with ordinary reality. As she walked down the street she had that rigid, wooden gait that people assume when they can hardly stand up and daren't make any superfluous movements. At home her interaction with us was limited to the subject of food and to the various arguments we put forward to make her see that sooner or later she'd collapse and that she couldn't survive like this. She was indifferent to all our reasoning. Now that she was on a complete fast she no longer experienced the screaming fits that had continued right up to her last sip of water. Now she was like a pillar of salt, quietly melting away, keeping its shape but dissolving slowly into nothingness. In the middle of all this, Marco, and his entry into junior school, was completely forgotten. Franco and I spent all our time – bar our actual teaching hours – clinging to each other, bewildered and terrified, in such a state of anguish that we thought we'd never come through it. With such lucidity as was still at our command, we went back over Marta's life experiences, and for the first time Franco really listened to me and tried to follow my reasoning. Now he realised what a lot of mistakes we'd made. What could we do to set things right?

One morning Franco came to pick me up from school. He wanted to talk and it seemed as if he suddenly understood what I'd been on about all these years. We thought back to the first wrong he'd ever done Marta. It was nothing to do with the scene he'd made because I'd named her Marta instead of calling her after his mother. It was his confiscation of the first toy she'd been given. She was only two days old, and Wanda had come to visit me in hospital. When she arrived she put a huge teddy bear into the baby's cot – it was bigger than Marta herself – and then she gazed at the little face, exclaiming with astonishment, 'You've given birth to yourself!'

Franco arrived shortly after Wanda, and as soon as he caught sight of the teddy bear he was horrified and said rudely to Wanda that it was wrong to give a little baby such a monster. He took the present out of the cot and flung it away. It sat in a cupboard for a month until the new godmother came on her next visit, carrying a doll. We gave her back the bear and Franco said approvingly of the doll, 'That's a proper present!'

In the years that followed the children had had all sorts of presents, but never a teddy bear. Marta had sometimes seen them in shop windows and expressed a wish for one, but teddy bears had become taboo so I'd always directed her attention elsewhere. This suddenly seemed a terrible thing to Franco and, almost in tears, he begged me, 'Let's go now, quick, and buy one – the biggest, most expensive, beautiful one we can find!' I followed him, in tears, in to the first toy shop we came across.

They had a teddy bear the size of a real bear, with a head three times the size of Marta's and a sweet, gentle face, sitting with his paws outstretched as if he were about to hug somebody against his soft, brown fur.

'That one!' said Franco without hesitating. Personally, I wouldn't have chosen one quite so large and conspicuous, but that is typical of Franco – he is absolutely unpredictable. So I raised no objections; I felt touched at the significance he attached to the gesture and I had some crazy hope that it might make a difference. We put the bear on Marta's bed while she was at school. It looked as if it were waiting for her – it was so big you could see it from the doorway. When Marta came home she seemed pleased with it and thanked us warmly, adding that we shouldn't have spent so much money. But there was no way she would come and eat anything and we felt more discouraged than ever. We forced ourselves to eat something: we had to keep going and we didn't want to give Marco the impression that his parents had joined the hunger strike too. But we didn't feel a bit hungry and by now cooking had become a nightmare to me. Still, I had to do it because we had to eat, although we swallowed our food quickly as if to hide the act from ourselves and, more important, we had to keep trying to persuade Marta to eat. She might capitulate at any moment and each time we sat down at the table we begged and implored her to join us.

One morning, in the middle of one of my lessons, I had a telephone call from Marta's headmaster. It was only ten days after the beginning of the new school term; to us those ten days had been an eternity. It seemed that Marta had been taken ill, and while she was half-conscious they'd given her a heart stimulant, which she had swallowed without realising. It must have been the signal that Franco and I were both fearing and yet hoping for. We could never have forced Marta to see a doctor or accept treatment unless something of the sort had happened, because it would have seemed like violence on our part. Since Franco had such an aversion to Nestore, we went to a psychoanalyst at the Mental Health Centre. Marta's headmaster was very understanding and concerned, and obviously felt personally involved. It was he who gave us the name of the doctor. We made an appointment for the same evening. Marta was unexpectedly docile and came with us unprotestingly. Perhaps she was aware that her obstinate resistance was leading her away from the goal she really sought – because it must have been a desire for liberation into life that she was trying to express, and not into death.

The doctor lived in a small villa in the suburbs. It was hard to make out what the house was like because it was already getting dark. We waited some time for the doctor, and when he arrived his appearance was reassuring. He had a pleasant face, penetrating eyes and a charming smile. No doubt his professional air had been acquired over the years, though he was still a fairly young man. He encouraged me to talk and I tried to give him an idea of Marta's background and the sort of life she'd led. I made an effort to be objective, but my conflicts with Franco were implicit in everything I said. Then he asked if he might speak privately with Marta. He concluded that the girl was quite willing to talk things over and that it was obvious she couldn't come to terms with the sort of life she was obliged to lead. The prolonged fast was only too easy to diagnose: it was a case of anorexia. He said that my cooperation was very valuable and gave him some hope that the problem might clear up quickly. I pointed out that there wasn't much time; Marta was very weak and had already collapsed once. He examined her and Marta didn't try to stop him. Indeed, she seemed to be in a different phase now. She behaved as if she didn't care about her body any more and it didn't matter what happened to it.

'Your heart's a bit weak, my girl!' the doctor said. 'If we don't give it some help, it won't be able to do its job.'

He prescribed some heart tablets and said she could take them without water if she couldn't bring herself to drink any. Marta said she would take them.

'But you ought to eat a little bit of food as well.'

'I can't.'

'Try, just a very little.'

'No.'

However, the doctor gave me some hope: he didn't seem to share my fear that the girl might die at any minute. He asked if he could meet her father and we made another appointment. Franco was in far more anguish this time than he had been when we'd had to take Marco to see Nestore. He looked conscience-striken, like a child who's been caught doing something wrong, and he listened quietly, without any attempt to justify himself. But finally he burst out:

'I just can't understand how I can be to blame for such a terrible thing! I loved my children more than anything else in the world – everything I did, I did for their own good. I tried to protect them from danger and defend them against anything bad. I gave my daughter everything she wanted, I adored her – how can she refuse life like this? How can she do this to herself – such an atrocious thing? How can she punish us like this?'

This was his defence and he clung to it grimly. He could hardly do otherwise, because the responsibility would have crushed him if he'd recognised it, and it had always been his way to blame other people rather than accept his own part in anything. I knew he was like that, but all I wanted now was for him to agree that, although we'd made mistakes, it was up to us from now on to find new paths and create new breathing spaces so that Marta could see that all was not yet lost. When Franco asked how we were going to persuade Marta to eat, neither the doctor nor I could think of anything except for us both to rethink our behaviour towards Marta. But Franco thought this was a waste of time; he felt overwhelmed and unable to imagine how he could go about such an operation.

The days went by. We talked to the doctor, first Marta and then Franco and I, because Marta wouldn't talk if her father was in the room. The fast continued, and Franco begged me to try anything I could think of. And I racked my brains – I never stopped thinking about it. By now Marta looked angular and stiff, all her movements seemed unnatural and it came back to me how often Franco had curbed her exuberance when she was a little girl and forced her to keep still.

'You see,' I said to him, 'Marta can hardly move now. She looks paralysed. Do you remember how many times you told her not to move, not to run, not to play with the ball? Now you've succeeded.' It was very cruel to say things like that to him now but I couldn't help it. I had suffered each time he'd curbed the children in the past, and now I was suffering as much as he was at the consequences.

'But I did it for her own good! I didn't want her to get hurt, that's all.'

'There's a way of loving that's worse than hating – it kills more surely.'

'You're a real bitch! Even at a time like this, you've got no pity for me.'

'Yes, I am a bitch! I'm a bitch for never finding the courage to stand up to you and make my own decisions, not even for my children's sake.'

'You are the one who's ruined them, always arguing with me! If you'd listened to me like other people's wives do, our children wouldn't be in this mess.'

It was terrible to tear each other to shreds like this, but our altercations were short-lived: we knew we had to concentrate on the problem itself.

'Suppose we take the children to play football? We could pretend we're just going for a walk and then take a ride out of town somewhere where there's some space. Then we'll get the ball out, and you can start kicking it around. Maybe Marta will join in.'

We knew it was a stupid idea, but all the talking with the doctor wasn't getting us anywhere, and we couldn't bear to do nothing. We planned it all carefully: Franco went and picked the children up from school and I went off to buy the ball, which I hid in my bag. When they arrived in a taxi, Franco suggested the outing over the intercom, as if it had just occurred to him because of the nice weather. We reached the gully – Franco couldn't think of anywhere better – and we went down to the dry river bed where there were more stones than grass. I got the ball out as if there were nothing unusual in it and Franco, awkward and unused to playing football, assumed the air of a fanatical sportsman. Marco, who was in on the secret, did his best to cooperate, but he was no footballer either. I even joined in myself, creaking and horribly unfit, kicking the ball wildly in all directions.

Marta watched us with an air of complete indifference. She didn't even look surprised.

'Come on, Marta, come and play!'

She made no reply and went and sat down on a boulder.

'Come on!'

'It's great, why don't you come?'

Marta said she was tired and wanted to go home. We all stood round her, trying to persuade her to stay. It was as if everything depended on this game – if we gave up, all would be lost. We pleaded with her, almost in tears, and pulled her arm, but she shook us off. In the end we went back to the waiting taxi. The taxi driver must have wondered what on earth those four people thought they were doing in the gully at that time of day, when everyone else was having lunch. Were they playing or arguing, and why would they spend so much money on a performance like that?

The complete fast went on and on, and we were out of our minds with worry. The doctor started saying that he couldn't be responsible for the case any longer. We'd have to go elsewhere. The girl's organism required help: she had kept going long enough as it was. I made her weigh herself every day – I hoped it would frighten her. All it did was give Marta a sort of macabre satisfaction at seeing how she was losing weight. She'd already dropped from fifty-four kilos to thirty-five. I decided to find a specialist who would get her into a clinic so as to keep her body alive somehow while we and the doctor grappled with her mind. We couldn't face a hospital.

I took her to an intern for a general examination. He agreed that something had to be done fast and, because he thought there might still be a physical origin to the phenomenon, he sent me to an endocrinologist. I asked this specialist, in secret, to take Marta into his private clinic, ostensibly for tests but really so that she could be fed intravenously. She hadn't eaten or drunk anything now for over two weeks and her whole metabolism had ground to a halt. She had to have something to keep her alive.

The endocrinologist examined Marta and then explained to her that she probably had some hormonal imbalance and that, in order to regulate her menstrual cycle, they'd have to do some tests and perhaps prescribe some treatment. Marta may have seen the disappearance of her periods as the loss of something precious. She was also alarmed by her dry, peeling skin: it looked like the first stages of scurvy. So she agreed to go into the clinic for a few days to get rid of these problems.

I went with her to the clinic and the professor started her treatment immediately. Marta spent long hours on an intravenous drip, interspersed with injections and nurses taking blood samples for tests. However, she never opened her mouth, not even to take any medicine. When she realised that she was surrounded by lots of people who didn't accept her refusal to eat, she became very defensive, and if anyone tried to force her to eat she got upset and shouted at them. In the end I implored the nursing staff to ignore her behaviour and pretend they didn't notice it. I ate the patient's meals myself, much to the amazement of the canteen women. Marta seemed more confident now that she had a lot of people concerned about her health and she was grateful to me. But sometimes she seemed more disturbed and uneasy than ever.

I stayed by her bedside all the time, knitting, and the idea of her lying there ill and me watching over her seemed to comfort her. Maybe it awoke in her distant memories of babyhood, before Marco was born, when I used to sit by her cot for hours, rocking her and singing lullabies just for her, or when I used to just stay near her, sewing or knitting, as I was doing now. I reflected that after Marco's arrival she'd never had me sitting by her bed like this any more, except briefly when she'd been ill. But she hadn't been ill very often. Who knows, perhaps that time when I was giving birth to Marco and she'd been ill, she'd missed me very badly? After that I was singing lullabies to Marco. I was taking care of her as well, but I'd often had my back turned to her and perhaps she'd felt less cared for than her little brother.

Now I seemed to be getting somewhere. I felt that Marta's mood was more positive and more inclined towards a healing process. I got her to talk as much as possible; I tried to decipher what she meant. Sometimes I'd throw in a comment in an attempt to lead the conversation round to more significant topics. In the afternoon Franco and Marco used to come and see her. So did our various friends and relations. It made the atmosphere more tense, but at least while Marta was surrounded by other people, all vying to give her advice and encouragement, I could grab a chance to see Marco. But he avoided me: he ran off down the corridors and it was obvious that he had no desire to talk to me. I begged Franco to spend as much time with him as he could while I was absent, even though my mother was there running the household. In the evenings Marta's drip was removed, and she would make herself pretty and sit on her bed, waiting for her doctor to arrive. He had special permission to come in and continue his sessions with her.

Then the doctor and I would try to reconstruct her past and understand what had happened. During one of these talks the old Barbie doll episode came up. Marta had talked about it with the doctor, but in a confused way. When Franco came to take my place, I went home and looked for the doll. I found the head carefully preserved in a box full of other dolls' heads. The body was in a pile of old toys abandoned in a cupboard. It looked as if when Marta saw her own body developing into that of a woman she had identified with the doll. Then, when her father had stopped her going out with her friends or meeting boys at parties – thus preventing the least opening up of her new sexuality – she had learned to turn inwards and hate this body that had brought her nothing but oppression. Perhaps she'd thrown the doll's body away as if she intended to ignore her own body. Then she'd set about starving her body back to its childish shape, freeing it from the womanly curves. This discovery made a very great impression on me.

Back in the clinic, I said casually to Marta, when everyone else had gone, 'Do you know, I was tidying up your room and I found Barbie!'

Marta looked at me in surprise, her attention immediately caught: 'But Barbie's broken, I haven't got her any more.'

'Well, yes, I only found her head. But her body must be around somewhere.'

She was silent. Then, with a look of timid supplication: 'Mummy, you know . . .'

'What?'

'I'd like to have another Barbie. That one's broken now.'

'If you want another one, we'll buy you one.'

'I do, but . . .'

'But what?'

'Daddy . . .'

'Daddy will happily buy you another one.'

'Would he really?'

'You wait and see. I'll phone him and he'll bring it for you.'

I rang him up, and in the afternoon Franco arrived with a parcel and handed it to Marta with the air of a penitent child hoping for forgiveness. Marta sat gazing at her doll for a long time. Meanwhile, out of her hearing, I tried to get Franco to recall this distant episode. I pointed out what implications it might have had in his daughter's mind. Franco could hardly remember the scene and was amazed that a such a trivial event could have such dramatic effects. I did my best to make him see that quite banal episodes can become highly significant if they come to represent a situation which has weighed very heavily on someone. It then becomes necessary to reconstruct the situation carefully down to the last detail in order to be able to understand what has happened.

We were so upset and confused, and under so much pressure to find a solution, that we tended to overrate the importance of episodes of this kind. Franco found it almost impossible to admit that there had been any repression, and so the doctor and I spent a great deal of time and energy trying to explain it and bring it all home to him. Perhaps this led us to exaggerate and distort the truth.

Anyway, Barbie really did become Marta's projected self. The doll represented what she wanted to be but could not, so for a while Marta had Barbie act out the life that she felt unable to lead herself. It took a lot of patience to use this symbolic figure to convince Marta that she could in fact make the doll's reality her own, if only she would fight to achieve it herself.

Franco, in his search for a solution – but also in his desire to lay the blame on someone else – came up with another theory. Perhaps the pregnancy of Marta's cousin Liliana was an important factor in her present mental state? After all, Marta had taken a lot of interest in the recent drama.

The doctor, when he heard this suggestion, seemed very interested. He consulted his books and said yes, that could have been the trigger. Maybe the girl identified with her cousin and felt her own inner self to be like a foetus, a foreign body. Perhaps she refused food so as to deprive this foetus of nourishment because she feared it and wanted it to die. I agreed that it might be one of the circles closing in on Marta, but I felt this so-called discovery was designed not so much to free Marta as to remove responsibility from Franco. He could thus lay the blame at his sister's door. And, sure enough, he went and threw scenes at his mother's house and then at his sister's, accusing her of being responsible for the whole tragedy and the probable death of his daughter.

I heard all this from Teresa, who was shattered and telephoned me to say that this was impossible, that she already had bad problems of her own and she couldn't bear this extra burden. I asked her to come and see us at the clinic, and when she came I told her my honest opinion. We didn't want to find scapegoats, we just wanted to get to the bottom of the situation and understand the dynamics involved. I told her I was sure that Marta's present state was the culmination of a long series of events – maybe the Liliana story was one of the last links in the chain, but I assured Teresa that neither I nor Marta herself held her family in any way responsible for the problems we were facing now. I asked her to get Liliana to come and visit her cousin. It would do Marta good to see how joyfully Liliana looked forward to the birth of her baby despite all the upsets and difficulties.

The doctor said this was an excellent idea, and he tried to calm Franco down when he objected. Franco, with his innate terror of sex, was horrified at the thought of his daughter setting eyes on her cousin's illegitimately swollen belly. He could hardly bear to look himself. But Liliana came, and Marta was pleased.

Despite all these efforts, the situation remained unchanged. Meanwhile, the senior consultant of the clinic announced that he could not carry out any tests because of the girl's abnormal physical condition. He said he didn't know what else he could do, since he did not treat patients with her particular illness. (What cast-iron compartments there are in our medical profession!) He asked us to go elsewhere.

We were no wiser than before. It was clear that Marta couldn't live on a drip for ever. The veins in her arms and even in her hands were surrounded by horrible bruises and it was increasingly difficult and painful to insert the needles. Marta was more and more restless. She no longer believed in the story of the tests she was supposed to be having, and the bottles of liquid flowing into her veins began to get on her nerves. In the end she regarded them with the same horror that she felt for ordinary food, and she began to weigh herself all the time. I had to keep fixing the scales so that they showed a lower weight, because if she had noticed an increase – even of a few grams – she'd really have gone mad.

And all this time we were paying incredible sums of money to the clinic, with no end in sight. So I decided to take her home. I made her promise solemnly that she would try to eat. The professor warned us not to neglect the matter because she was in a very dangerous physical condition. I asked him to have a word with Marta, and he did so. He also prescribed a light diet for her, as if this were the result of all the tests.

We took her home, but there was no change at all. Our own doctor also announced that he could no longer be responsible for the case. Franco and all the other members of the family screamed accusations at each other. I called a woman doctor in Milan who was considered to be the greatest European expert on anorexia. I had a talk with her, but nothing practical came of it because she couldn't give me an appointment for three months. She said we would have to bring the whole family, including both sets of grandparents and anyone else who was directly involved in our family life. Three months meant certain death, so we'd have to find somebody else.

I got in touch with Wanda in Rome. She knew one of the city's leading lights in the medical world and as a special favour this doctor gave us an appointment for two days hence, at the Child Psychiatry Department of the Rome Polyclinic. It was very difficult to persuade Marta to undertake this journey. She was so weak by now – all she wanted was to be left in peace. I spent the two days before we set off making a rag doll to give Wanda's little girl. There was nothing else I could do, and I couldn't sit idle. My mother did all the housework and cooking. Marco didn't seem to want to talk to me and I hadn't the energy to draw him out. Marta was shut in her tragic silence. At last it was time to leave. Franco, Marta and I set off by car, with a friend of Franco's driving. Marta spent the whole trip spitting saliva into her handkerchief: by now she couldn't even swallow her own saliva.

It was dusk when we reached Rome. Franco went off to fill in all the forms necessary for urgent hospital admission, and by the time we got into the department it was quite dark. They said there was no question of my being allowed to stay too. I asked if I could just go in for a moment to see where she'd be and talk to the doctor. Grumbling and reluctant, they let me through; we went down two long corridors, past wards with reddish lighting where we could see children wandering around like small ghosts. They were all ages – mongols, spastics, children with every degree of mental subnormality. Their faces were blank, their round eyes completely stupefied; they moved convulsively or else very, very slowly, and the nurse who watched them were hard-faced, like jailors. At the end of the wing the nurse turned on a dim light and we saw a small room with two little rusty, iron beds. When we were alone Marta flung herself down on one of the little beds, which was too short for her, and began to sob her heart out.

'I knew I couldn't trust you; you're going to leave me here! You want to get rid of me! You don't care if they slit my throat. I warn you, I won't let them kill me. I'll bang my head against this bedhead until I smash it in. I will! I swear it!'

'No, Marta, don't think that! I'll never go off and leave you. We came to see the professor we made an appointment with. Don't be frightened, I promise nothing will happen to you. Your parents are here with you and they're looking after you.'

'It's not true. I don't believe you. In a minute they'll send you away and I'll never get out of here alive.'

'No. Calm down – it'll be all right, you'll see.'

The food trolley arrived. They wanted to dish us out a tin plateful of brown broth from a huge aluminium container. I told them we didn't want anything, but then I let them give me an apple so as not to offend them. Two interminable hours passed. I had grown used to the constant tension and anxiety, but this waiting was worse than anything. Finally a junior doctor arrived and asked us into the nurses' office to take down the medical history. I replied to her questions and then I asked what time the professor would arrive.

'The professor? He's gone to Germany for a conference. He'll be back next week. We'll do all the tests in the meantime.'

Marta shot me a look of terror.

'No,' I said firmly. 'In that case we won't wait.'

'What on earth do you mean? You've asked for an urgent admission to the clinic. Your daughter is seriously ill – you just can't take the responsibility . . .'

'I take all the responsibility. I won't leave my daughter here for one minute.'

The doctor looked at me. She was amazed and offended. 'Your daughter will be perfectly well cared for. Whatever do you imagine will happen to her?'

'I don't imagine anything. All I know is that I'm taking her out of here. Look, please just tell me what the formalities are.'

'All right.' She wrote something on a form. 'Sign this declaration.'

I signed. She gave me some more forms to fill in, and told me which office to take them to.

I ran to the main entrance. Franco was hanging round there like a stray dog. I told him quickly what I wanted to do, and he took the forms and went to give them in. Then I phoned Wanda, and asked her if she'd come and pick us up. I explained that it was no good at the Polyclinic and that we'd have to try and think of something else. Wanda arrived an hour later: Franco and I were still trying to decide whether to go home or stay in Rome and try to find some alternative.

'You're here in Rome now. Try some other doctor. There's nothing you can do back home anyway.'

That was true.

'Stay at my house. We'll try and find a friend of mine that you can consult.'

So Franco set off for home and Marta and I went back with Wanda. It was miserable for us, in that state, to try and fit into a normal family life. Our hosts did their best to make us, feel at home, even though they realised that we existed on a very different plane. Wanda's house was really beautiful and Marta loved it. When she saw the two children playing with the dog and cat, she said she'd always wanted a dog. Naturally, she didn't touch any food, and she continued to spit out her saliva, which was increasingly acid.

Wanda and Dino hardly knew how to help me. After we'd put the children to bed, and Marta had gone to sleep in the guest room, we tried to take stock of the situation and made a few phone calls. The only possibility that emerged was yet another private clinic, more tests and then – what? We'd already been through all that in Bari, and time was short now. I'd promised Marta that I wouldn't leave her alone anywhere and that made it all the more difficult to go to a private clinic. We had already paid out far more than we could afford at the previous place. Anyway, I felt strongly that I ought not to leave her because I was the one who had lived alongside her and had been able to observe her experiences. And if only we could find the starting point, these observations might enable us to unravel the knot.

Wanda had a friend who was a psychiatrist, and he agreed that this inner search was the only way forward. He thought it was important for Marta to carry on talking to her own doctor, since she seemed so willing to cooperate with him. So I decided to go home the next day, on the afternoon fast train. I had a long talk with Wanda, which helped me to focus on elements in the story that I hadn't thought about before. Marta had said she would like to have a dog. Franco had always loathed dogs because he was scared of them, and he'd always warned the children not to go near them – not to go near any animals in fact. Another case of father saying no.

'How about if she had a puppy to look after?' said Wanda. 'She'd have to give it food and water, and maybe that would encourage her to start taking nourishment herself. Maybe she'd feel the responsibility for her own life more – she might see it as a sort of duty: she'd see that her life is in her own hands just like the puppy's.'

I didn't know how she'd take it. A few months ago it might have been a new outlet for her, but then a few months ago it would have been out of the question to give her a puppy. We could but try: in the present position we couldn't afford to ignore any idea that might work. We decided that we'd try and buy a little poodle the next morning. Then I went to bed, and lay there wide awake listening to Marta's breathing. It had kept me awake for nights – I was tortured by the idea that it might suddenly just stop.

I couldn't get to sleep for thinking about the nightmarish scenes we'd witnessed in the Polyclinic. I reflected that however badly off we were, at least we were more fortunate than those poor children who had finished up in that concentration camp of a hospital. I couldn't bear to think of so much misery and I felt the deep, muffled anger that was the only strength I had left. Next morning, when Marta woke up, she gazed round the room with its low sofas piled with cushions, the countrified fireplace, the shelves full of books and the little rugs.

'I wish I had a house like this!' she said.

'When you're old enough to live by yourself and earn a living, you'll be able to have a house and decorate it just as you please.'

'Yes, I'd do it just like this.'

We got ready to go out. Marta looked extremely weak. She could barely stand upright, and as we went downstairs she had a nasty tumble. Luckily she wasn't hurt. We drove through the streets of Rome, and Wanda talked away about all sorts of things – but she spoke with a *joie de vivre* that was really infectious, and I responded in the same spirit, aware that Marta was listening in silence, and that she might grasp our message – that all this could be hers if only she'd find the strength to take it. After a while Wanda pulled up outside a pet shop and asked us to wait a few minutes. She came out bearing a two-month-old poodle puppy. Its coat was black and curly, its two liquid eyes shining with life. She deposited it on Marta's lap. 'Here you are,' she said, 'he's yours.'

Then she explained to Marta how to look after it: what to feed it, how often, how to housetrain it, and what vaccinations it ought to have. It sounded like a full-time job all right. Marta looked dazed. Her facial expressions were so infrequent and minimal now that it was hard to tell if she was pleased with the present or frightened – not frightened of the puppy but of the responsibility of looking after it. She was so weak that it might be too much of an effort for her. Wanda dropped us off at a park while she went to pick her children up from school. Marta tried to keep up with the puppy, who pulled at the lead and ran hither and thither looking for his lost mother and brothers, but she looked more and more cross and tired. I didn't know what to do to help her. Everything I said to try and encourage her to open up towards life, which streamed busily around us, disappeared as if into a void.

At lunchtime I noticed that she was staggering – she couldn't walk properly any more – and I broke down.

'Look Marta,' I said, 'from now on, if you don't eat, I won't either: then we'll both die.'

Her reaction was unexpected. 'Oh, Mummy,' she cried, 'please don't do that to me: if you don't eat, I'll die!'

The minute the words were out, I suddenly felt quite sure that she had regressed to a pre-birth stage, when the foetus is nourished by the mother. 'Do you realise what you're saying? It's ridiculous! You're not inside me – there's no umbilical cord between us. You can't live on what I eat. If I eat and you carry on not eating, you'll die – you'll really die. You're dying now.'

But she was completely out of control. She continued to beg me to help her, saying that only I could do it, and only in this particular way. She was deaf to any reasoning or logic.

So it looked as if Marta had within her a great will to live, but was unable to express it, however much she tried. In her own way she was asking me to hang on, so that I could help her find the way through. So I went and ate something, although by this time anything I ate tasted so bitter to me that I could hardly swallow.

Wanda and Dino were extremely distressed at being unable to help us. During the long return journey with Marta and the puppy, who slept on her knee, I tried to think what else I could do to try and save her. After the experience at the Rome Polyclinic, how would we ever persuade her to go into a hospital again? But she was in such a bad state now that she urgently needed medical help – intravenous feeding, blood transfusions and cardiotonic drugs. As soon as we got home I tried to get hold of our doctor, but he had gone to Bologna. Then I telephoned Cristina: she was a nurse who worked in the clinic where Marta had been. She and I had become friends, and I asked her to phone me the next day and pretend that Marta needed to come in for one small test to complete the series she'd already had.

I went across the road to Luciano's house to make these phone calls so that Marta couldn't overhear me. The air in our house was unbreathable: Marta hadn't the strength to get up and the puppy was wandering from room to room, whining and tearing everything he found to bits. He left his little round puppy puddles everywhere. My mother and Franco were furious about the purchase of this puppy, and I too realised that the idea wasn't going to work: Marta felt nothing but irritation for the poor little animal.

At last Cristina phoned, and I told Marta that we had to go round to the clinic just to do a blood test, so she'd have to make an effort and get up. I helped her dress and then I hid her pyjamas in my bag and told my mother to get Franco to come on after me with the little suitcase that I'd packed. We took a taxi to the clinic. Cristina had got a room ready for us. It was a cold, wet November day, and when Marta had climbed into bed I looked at her and all of a sudden I realised how far gone she was.

Cristina was shocked. 'Why have you waited so long?' she asked. 'Can't you see that she's dying.'

The doctors who rushed to examine her confirmed that she was in a cachexic and precomatose condition. She was given emergency treatment and before long she fell into a torpor. At least the tension disappeared and she looked more relaxed now.

'I can't understand it,' said Cristina. 'Is there really no way to deal with this?'

'You tell me,' I replied, anguished. 'I've tried everything and nothing has worked, it's all gone wrong. I don't want to lose her like this!'

'Now calm down, you can't do anything now. If you want to save her you must let other people take over. Will you consent to a psychiatric consultation? I will make the arrangements, but you must promise to do whatever they advise.'

'Of course, why shouldn't I? Have I gone against advice so far?'

'Would you agree to your daughter being transferred to the Psychiatric Hospital if that's what they advise?'

'The Psychiatric Hospital? Well – if . . . if it would help.'

'How about your husband?'

'Yes, I suppose my husband would agree . . .'

'We have to request a consultation anyway, because we can't keep a patient in such a serious condition here in the clinic – it would be a very great responsibility.'

'Please do whatever is necessary, Cristina!'

The doctors who had been called in for the consultation arrived in the early afternoon and shut themselves in Marta's room. Franco and I were shut out like intruders. We paced up and down the deserted corridors, unable to look each other in the eye, afraid to see reflected there the bewilderment we both felt. After what seemed an eternity they came out again. The senior doctor came over to speak to us.

'The girl is very seriously ill,' he said. 'She must be admitted to our department immediately.'

He looked at us as if we were wicked parents who might kill their own daughter if she wasn't removed post haste. And, looked at from the outside, that was in fact how things were.

'All right. Tell us what to do and we'll do it.'

'We will take care of everything from now on. All you have to do is leave it to us. That's the only thing you can do now to help your daughter.'

Then they forgot about us and began to talk urgently amongst themselves in low voices. We took the opportunity to slip surreptitiously into Marta's room. She lay there, her face white against the mass of dark hair spread over the pillow. An intravenous drip slowly emptied drugs into her arm. Franco sobbed like a frightened child; I stood there like a figure carved out of stone, wanting to cry. But I had to carry on, I had to fight, I couldn't let go now.

All that night I watched over Marta, making sure that the drip worked and listening to her breathing. It was almost imperceptible and often I leant over her sleeping face so as to feel her breath. By dawn my head was bursting. Thoughts ran through my mind endlessly, but I knew they couldn't change the real situation: I had lost control over it. And sure enough, a bustle of activity began as they organised Marta's transfer to the Psychiatric Hospital. Marta suddenly seemed to realise what was going on around her and watched everything intently. The ambulance arrived, and I told her as calmly as I could that she was very ill and so they had to transfer her to another ward. I told her not to worry — everything would be all right and they would save her. Two nurses lifted her on to a stretcher, took her down in the elevator and carried her into the waiting ambulance. I slipped in too. I sat next to Marta and held her hand. She looked at me trustingly and I tried to reassure her. We drove across to the hospital with the siren screaming, and I felt as if that scream called the whole city to share in this dramatic rescue. Franco was already there, going through the formalities for urgent hospital admission. The little stretcher now seemed to belong to a different world, out of our reach, even though we followed in its wake along interminable corridors, through waiting rooms and up and down flights of stairs. We reached the ward and they put the stretcher down. A crowd of patients in their dressing gowns gathered round to see. They looked down at Marta with a mixture of pity and curiosity. Marta looked back at them with big, dark eyes.

'Oh, look! It's a little girl!'

'Isn't she pretty!'

'Poor little thing, what's the matter with her?'

They were motherly and kind, despite their dazed, drugged faces. They said kind words to me, too.

'You look just like your little girl!'

Little girl! Yes, lying there now, with her innocent, vulnerable little face, she did look like a child. I began to make friends with the patients, telling them my story so they would understand, and some of the more lucid women tried to comfort me. They told me not to worry, that they would look after the 'little girl' and make sure that nobody did anything to hurt her. They put Marta in a room with a young country woman suffering from depression who promised me that she would look after Marta as if she were her own daughter.

Then two young doctors came to summon Franco and me. They wanted to take down the medical history and they started asking questions. I replied and tried to explain, until one of the doctors interrupted me: 'But, Signora, why don't you let your husband do the talking?' Franco apologised for me: 'She knows the story better than I do – she can be more help to you.'

'The Signora sees things from her point of view. It would be much better if you would give us your version of the matter.'

Franco tried to comply, but he was unsure of himself and kept turning to me for support.

'My dear sir, surely you must have your own ideas on the subject. Don't keep looking at your wife. Tell us what you think.'

Franco found it very difficult to do as he was asked and, instead of recounting the facts, he began protesting that he had always had the girl's good at heart and had never imagined that he could hurt her. I couldn't help intervening.

'It is clear that your daughter is in this condition because of the mistakes that you have made. You, as the father, have failed to insist on obedience, and you, as the mother, have not kept the rules.'

'What rules? Isn't it the duty of both parents to bring up

their children?'

'Yes, but it's up to the father to decide how it should be done. It's the mother's place to do it.'

'And what if the father makes mistakes?'

'The father cannot make mistakes because he is the repository of the social customs and values that his own upbringing has entrusted to him.'

'And what if these rules are based on principles I can't accept?'

'Then your duty is quite clear: even if you don't think they are right, you must accept them for your children's sake. That is the contract that you made when you married. You are therefore outside the norm.'

To my surprise, Franco leapt to my defence: 'My wife is an intelligent woman, and there are a lot of things that I now see she was right about.'

'That is exactly where you made your mistake. You let your wife get the better of you and you lost your grip on the situation. You failed to lay down the law and so you left your daughter without any clear guidelines as to what is right and wrong.'

After a bit more along these lines they brought our interview to a close by saying that we should now make an effort to repair the damage we'd done by staying away and leaving everything to them.

'Signora, we want you to make a big effort not to come near your daughter until we give you permission.'

How could I refuse? It was true that our love had not been able to cure Marta and now she needed professional help.

'All right,' I said. 'You take over. Please.'

'We shall do everything we can. Now, don't worry, go home and try to forget that your daughter is here.'

But Marta was already shouting for me because she didn't know where I'd gone. Her screams were desperate and she was trying to get out of bed. The kind-hearted women tried to calm her down, and one of them came to call me.

'The Signora has to go now,' said the doctor.

The woman begged for me: 'Just for a minute!'

He hesitated and then, hearing the terrible screams, he said irritably: 'All right. Just one minute. And explain to your daughter that you can't stay here and she's just got to put up with your absence.'

I ran into the room and Marta clung to me. 'Mummy, don't leave me, you can't, I can't bear it if you do!'

I tried to disengage her arms and make her lie down. 'Relax,' I said, trying to speak calmly and quietly. 'You're very ill now, and they have to save you. I can't stay with you but I'll come and see you every day. You must promise to get better. There are all these kind people to keep you company.'

'Come along now, Signora,' said the doctor.

And they were already coming into the room with feeding tubes and all sorts of other equipment.

'Goodbye! I'll come tomorrow.'

'No, Mummy, no! Help! They're going to kill me!'

'I'll come tomorrow afternoon to see how you are.'

'Mummy! Mummy!'

They dragged me out and held Marta down as she stretched out her arms to me. They shut the door, and Marta's screams became animal-like – it sounded as though they were cutting her throat. Franco, sobbing, took my arm and pulled me away. I stumbled down the corridor, holding on to the wall. We went downstairs and along more corridors, but I could still hear Marta screaming for me. Her screams grew more distant, but no less desperate: it sounded like an animal being dragged to the slaughterhouse. A young, blond doctor, tall and self-confident, caught sight of me – he was the ward's senior doctor and he moved like a god in his little kingdom.

'Ah, Signora, come into my office for a moment, please.'

He waved us into his room. Then he explained that I must resign myself, that my daughter's illness was incurable. He assured me that although I now seemed so determined to keep my daughter, I would soon get tired of her and come and abandon her here, as so many other mothers had done. The girl would become institutionalised – hospital was the only place for her. I looked at him, dumbstruck, and shook my head – no, no. With what breath I still had, I told him I would fight and fight until I had untied all the knots in my daughter's mind – I would persevere, I would undo them one by one, even if it took me the rest of my life.

'In that case,' he said, 'you may perhaps be successful. But my experience leads me to believe the contrary. I think you will come to accept the situation – common sense will prevail and you will resume your normal life with the rest of your family.'

'But what would my family mean to me if I lost my daughter? I couldn't do that!'

'Try and think of your daughter as dead.'

I wanted to jump on him and smash him, sitting there in his armchair with his air of paternalistic complacency, pretending to offer sympathy while he murdered me. I got up and – because I knew he had the power – I asked him, please could I have permission to visit my daughter?

'As few visits as possible, Signora. I'm making an exception for you but mind you don't abuse your privilege. Otherwise I'll forbid you to enter the ward.'

'All right. I'll be discreet and I will try and help.'

'There's a good woman!'

But I could see that my help was the last thing he wanted. He thought I was a silly little woman who didn't know what she was talking about.

I had been forced into submission, but somehow I would find a way through: I had to fight. I left the hospital, looking devastated, but in my heart I was committed to my struggle. It was terrible to go home without Marta. I felt a sense of rejection towards everything and everyone: the faces of Marco and my mother as they greeted us, the furniture, the objects in the house – it all seemed alien. I lay on my bed and wept.

'I want to die,' I cried, 'I just want to die!'

Marco came and put his arm round me. The tears streamed down his face and he said: 'No, Mummy, please don't die. Live for me, promise you'll live for my sake.'

He was so forlorn, I held him close to me. I reassured him that I would indeed live for him, that he was the only person who could keep me going, but that I had to save his sister or I couldn't be a mother to him either.

My days were unreal. I couldn't sleep at night, and in the

morning I used to get up and go out into the streets, leaving everything in the house as it was. I felt like a half-developed larva. I was one – I could see it in the eyes of the passers-by. They looked at me as though I wasn't one of them. I'd reach the hospital and wander round the ground floor corridors, waiting for someone to leave the big glass door open and unguarded so I could get up to the first floor. Sometimes I waited for hours. In the end I'd manage to slip upstairs, and then I'd have another wait outside the doors of Marta's ward. I watched people's shadows moving behind the opaque glass. The door opened: it was visiting time and I could go in. The nurses would start protesting that I wasn't really supposed to . . . But I distributed tips to them and gradually they all turned a blind eye.

Marta was transformed: even on my first visit I found her calm and sleepy, her face bruised from the fight, with a tube taped in her nose. She looked at me as if I belonged to another world, and a nurse said triumphantly to me:

'Look how calm your daughter is, Signora. She's a good girl now and she knows she's got to do as she's told. Do you know, yesterday we got half a litre of milk and two beaten eggs down her! And today we gave her soup with biscuits dissolved in it, and she took every last drop.'

I thought how violently they must have treated her to get so much food into her. But I pretended to be pleased. The minute we were alone, the look in Marta's eyes became more intense and she whispered:

'Mummy, do you know what they did to me? They strapped me down and tied my arms to the bed and then they forced this thing up my nose – it hurt so much – and then they poured all that stuff into my stomach. I screamed until I nearly lost my voice. Now they say that if I'm good they'll take this thing out, this tube, and I'm trying to do what they say so they'll take it out quickly, because it hurts. I can't bear it.'

'Little love, I did everything I could think of to stop things going so far. But can you see that you were so ill that if I'd just waited for you to eat, I'd have let you die?'

She nodded and seemed convinced. 'But now tell them I'll eat by myself – tell them to take this thing out now.'

I called the nurse.

'You've got to show the professor that you'll eat food properly first. Then he will give orders for the tube to be removed.'

'Do you understand? Try and show him you're eating.'

The next day she had eaten some food, but the tube was still there and her nose looked even more swollen and bruised.

I went and spoke to the sister.

'You promised her that you would take the tube out as soon as she ate by herself.'

'The professor wants to be quite sure that she will continue to do as she's told.'

'But you promised!'

'She'll have to wait.'

I tried to comfort Marta. I told her to try and be patient, but as a matter of fact she was incredibly docile and submissive, quite unlike her usual self.

'What are you giving her?'

'Nothing, just a few tranquillisers to keep her quiet. Don't worry, they won't hurt her.'

But I did worry, because it was clear to me that their concept of treatment was to heap violence and oppression on minds and bodies already damaged by the violence and oppression they had suffered at the hands of their families and of society at large. I couldn't believe this was the best way to restore confidence and the will to live in those who'd lost it. The goal seemed to be to reduce these people to submissive, unprotesting patients who would suffer anything for the sake of survival: there seemed no question of their living a life worthy of the name. But I couldn't say anything, even to Marta. I just enjoined her to do everything they told her without protest so that I could get her out of there as fast as possible. And now that she was eating again, they removed the feeding tube. The professor had heard about my frequent visits and had peremptorily forbidden me to enter the ward, but Marta began blackmailing everyone so that she could see me: she said she'd only eat if it was I who gave her the food. At this the professor wanted to put her back on the tube, but his junior assistants persuaded him to let me in and so I was given permission to come in at lunch- and suppertime.

Now that Marta felt less physically repressed she grew bolder and began to talk more openly. She even argued intelligently with the professor and the other doctors. A few of the more sensitive doctors were thus encouraged to take a more flexible line and tried to part company with the professor's rigid policy on her case. He was forced to make various concessions, but he was not used to having his authority questioned in this manner and his response to the threat was to raise the level of Marta's sedation. He chose more sophisticated drugs so that, although she remained awake and lucid, her behaviour became more subdued and docile. I soon noticed the change: I now found her running about the ward like a good little dog, willing and helpful.

She had also started to walk about obsessively all day long so as to burn up calories and avoid gaining weight. At this point I began to think how I could get her away from the hospital treatment. It had certainly re-established her physic- al health, but it had done nothing to heal the cause of her illness. I told the professor that I was in touch with the woman specialist in Milan. He obviously had a lot of respect for her, and I got him to promise that as soon as I had an appointment for Marta, he would give her permission to go to Milan. It was not true, but the professor was too arrogant to imagine that anyone would dare lie to him, and so he believed me.

Of course, I was caught between my conviction that Marta shouldn't be in that hospital and my fear that if she came out she might regress to the point where I'd have to take her back to that frightening institution. There was no one to whom I could turn for help, except our doctor: he was willing to resume his talks with Marta, but he couldn't guarantee success. Then one day I arrived in Marta's ward and the nurses and patients told me that she had made a scene in front of everybody, accusing the professor of running a Nazi concentration camp. She had proclaimed that his methods were reactionary and repressive – and apparently everyone present had loudly agreed with her. She was a heroine. The heroine herself had been swiftly dealt with: she lay in her bed, drugged to the eyeballs, and I could hardly get through to her at all. At last she recognised me and a message came through from her besieged mind:

'Mummy, get me out of here, these people are killing me. Today I realised that they're drugging me.'

All my doubts vanished, and I put my plan in action. I went to see the professor and told him politely that I had an appointment in Milan for four o'clock the day after tomorrow. I asked him what procedure I should follow. All unsuspecting, he informed me that tomorrow I would have to sign a declaration to the effect that the girl was going out, at my request, to see a Milan specialist and that I undertook to bring her back as soon as possible. Then I could take my daughter out, on condition that I made sure she continued her medication. He wrote down exactly which pills she should take.

I got the house ready for her homecoming. I put some new furniture in her room, which made it cosier. We also cheered the house up, polishing and cleaning and even changing the worn upholstery on the armchairs. I asked Marco and Franco and my mother to help me by trying not to let Marta feel a stranger: we had to help her feel part of the family again after her traumatic experience.

All the aunts and uncles and several friends had been to see her in hospital, so she knew she was loved and wanted back home. Marco came with me to fetch her, and a friend of Franco's drove us there. He was a kind, good friend from Franco's political party who was very close to us. Marta was dazed from all the drugs, and I had to wait quite a while until she came out of her stupor. I had brought her the same clothes that she'd been wearing when she'd gone into hospital.

Back home, Franco and her grandmother were waiting to welcome her. So was Gulliver, the poodle: he was increasingly troublesome and excitable and when he saw Marta he seemed to recognise her as his real mistress and gave a great display of affection. Although she felt fuzzy, Marta examined every corner of the house with delight. I had talked to her over the last few days and tried to give her the feeling that her home was a warm, protective refuge and that she would get better there. Then we sat down to the simple lunch that my mother had made – the food was good but nothing special. No one was very expansive or natural – perhaps they were afraid of saying the wrong thing, or maybe everyone was intent on looking at Marta sideways to see what someone was like after they'd been 'put away'. Marta seemed too doped to notice anything unusual. She concentrated on eating small mouthfuls carefully and unenthusiastically. At the end of the meal she insisted on clearing the table and washing up and told her grandmother and me to go and have a rest.

My mother was most impressed. 'Did you see that!' she said to me when we were in the bedroom. 'Those people have re-educated her – they've got her doing the sort of jobs that you should have taught her.'

I disagreed. 'I deliberately didn't teach her those jobs because I don't believe that girls should be brought up to do the housework: either both sexes or nobody.'

'And so you had help from nobody.'

'But I tried to make everyone see the need for coopera-tion.'

'And look where it got you! Nobody saw the need and you did all the work.'

'That's because of the general attitude in our society. If this whole drama hadn't happened, I should have managed to communicate the right attitude in the end.'

'Huh!' said my mother. 'It's probably because you never helped me at home – you were always at your grandmother's. It was the boys who helped around the house.'

'Maybe that's it. I just think it's better to teach all children the same things. Especially nowadays when most women work outside the home. Why should they do all the housework as well?

I didn't feel good about Marta's sudden willingness to do housework. It seemed to me to be a sign of institutional re-education, an attempt to bring her into line in a manner which I had been at pains to avoid. And there was something else, too, that I found as alarming as her former refusal to eat. Marta herself had seen it coming and had seemed to be aware of the danger. On one of the last few days in hospital

110

she'd said to me:

'Mummy, something terrible is happening to me: I have to keep walking, all the time, even when I'm exhausted and want to rest.'

She never sat down when we were at home, except to eat. And even then she sat on the edge of her chair, as if she could hardly wait to get up again. She wanted to go out both morning and afternoon, so naturally I went with her. We covered miles, walking down street after street completely at random until I was worn out. I realised that Marta wasn't enjoying these marathons either – she felt forced to keep going; she could help herself, even though it went against her very survival instinct. When she came home, instead of eating a hearty meal, as anyone else would after such strenuous activity, she just picked at her food as usual. She never relaxed, she seemed only intent on consuming every last gram of energy she had.

I thought this symptom was as bad as the fasting. Her behaviour was obviously connected with being forced to eat. She had only eaten out of fear – fear of the tubes in her nose, the blood transfusions and drips – and now her mind had found another path towards freedom. Because it was clear by now that Marta's self-destructive processes were not designed to lead to her death: however abnormal the path, her search was for the freedom, independence and self-expression that had been systematically crushed both by society and by her family.

Our doctor also realised that she was on the downhill path again. He had resumed his sessions with her, but nothing came of them now because Marta had built up so much resentment against the whole medical profession and its methods, she didn't talk much with me either, and she gradually shut herself off again. She was like someone holding a fortress. Her relationship with other people – friends and family – was formal and polite, and she still seemed extraordinarily docile and submissive.

One evening I got a real shock. One of Marta's uncles came to see us. He was Franco's youngest brother and he was closer to us than the others. He found Marta ironing when he arrived.

'There's a good girl!' he said. 'I'm glad to see you learning to be a clever little housewife. Remember your uncle's advice: if you want your husband to appreciate you, you must iron his shirts nicely. The secret is to iron the collar and cuffs perfectly – and the shirt-front. The rest doesn't matter quite so much.'

Then he added that her husband would reward her by taking her to lots of lovely parties and giving her pretty dresses. Marta listened to all this quietly and submissively, with an artificial smile on her lips. But her eyes showed her bewilderment and she seemed to recede into the distance. I had the feeling that this was the danger she scented, this was what she wanted to escape. All she saw before her was the traditional role of women, the golden cage of great sacrifices and minimal rewards. My conviction that this was at the heart of the matter grew, and I felt sure that this was the area I had to work on. But everyone was pushing in the opposite direction and even Marta herself seemed intent on fulfilling the role that I'd rejected for her. And indeed, I was reproached on all sides for my inadequate mothering.

Even the doctor – who had decided to emulate the Milan expert and wanted sessions with the whole family now – seemed to wish to concentrate on me. He tried to persuade me that I ought to redefine my role: I ought to try and be more docile and submissive, and pay more attention to my appearance and my clothes. I ought to limit myself to the traditional female areas – in short, I should stop being myself and give up the world that I'd created for myself by my own work and thought.

He did have a certain amount of success with me at first, because I was so drained by the struggle of the last few months. I felt as if no one would help: everyone seemed set on gently convincing me that I should dedicate my life to looking after other people instead of trying to think. Marta was slipping backwards fast. What she ate was already inadequate and she was eating less every day. Recently I'd decided to gradually cut out all the various drugs she'd been prescribed except for the reconstituent injections. Only a few days before, I'd stopped giving her the pills which changed her mood because I thought it was unproductive for her to feel artificially optimistic and cheerful: all it did was encourage her to behave like a willing housewife. She herself had wished to discontinue them, partly because she realised she was obeying orders like a robot and partly because in order to take the pills she had to drink and she didn't like drinking between meals now.

It was this reappearance of the anorexia – although it wasn't total anorexia – that made me so vulnerable. Everyone, including the doctor, thought I ought to give in now and admit I'd been wrong. I should resign myself to the traditional role of wife and mother and stop asserting myself. I could expect just a few concessions to emancipation from my husband, in consideration of the prevailing progressive climate! I was sure that Marta's regression was due to her sense of doom, her feeling that her real personality was being suffocated so that she would become a socially conditioned puppet. But I couldn't express this knowledge in words or logical theories – it was an intuitive feeling that came to me gradually. We were now having family sessions with our doctor and this underlying feeling of mine complicated and upset our discussions so that our sessions were a real battleground.

These sessions were certainly positive, although not perhaps in the way that the doctor intended at the time. (After his experience with us, he began a whole rethinking process.) In the presence of this fifth character, the doctor, who acted as mediator and arbitrator, the other four characters – who lived shut off in their private worlds at home and maintained formal relationships with each other – were able to peel off the layers and expose their feelings, thoughts, impressions and dreams. Marco, Marta and I were fairly spontaneous and uninhibited, but Franco was very defensive. In the past he'd been the most outspoken member of the family and very spontaneous in his self-expression, but now he found it hard to say what he felt. He seemed anxious to defend himself against the attack on his traditional role as the patriarchal guardian of social and moral values.

Strangely enough, our discussions didn't focus on Marta – whose problems we now all tacitly agreed not to mention – but on Marco. The boy had taken heed of Marta's warning and Marta's experience and, now that his mother and father were busy with other problems, he used this holiday from parental supervision to carve out an independent life for himself, something that would have been unthinkable before. He was fascinated by the world of his schoolmates: they were almost all working-class kids, who worshipped physical strength and power and despised any sort of culture, school-orientated or otherwise. So Marco had given up all reading, flung aside his vests and all the other asthmatic precautions and gone off into the streets of the city. Now he saw everything with new eyes – the eyes of someone in control of his own life, with no adult protection or restraint. He went wherever he liked, he ran when he wanted to run, and made friends with whomsoever he saw fit.

He returned from these forays into the city looking exhilarated, his long, curly hair wild and uncombed, his shirt unbuttoned and his coat hanging casually open. He'd grown taller and leaner and he looked like a real street urchin, a Gavroche from Hugo's *Les Miserables*. I felt great tenderness for him and I recognised myself in him as well, because at his age I had also run wild through the streets with my brothers and all the local kids, unafraid and adventurous. But Franco trembled for him, he thought the thousand dangers of the city streets would overwhelm him, and he saw all sorts of imaginable and unimaginable terrors. Franco couldn't bear the shame of seeing Marco mixing with the bad lads at school and neglecting his appearance. The false sympathy of his colleagues made it worse. They were delighted to see such an example of family degeneration and were quick to point out to Franco the bad effects of his Marxist, anti-clerical ideology.

Franco would come home confused and frustrated and get mad with Marco, and thus Marco became the focal point of our discussions. Franco accepted the criticism of his so-called friends and said that Marco's behaviour was intolerable, and that he as a father had the right and the duty to put a stop to his son's conduct. I agreed that Marco's behaviour was excessive, but it seemed to me to be the natural reaction to his strict upbringing, and I thought that if we didn't make a drama out of it, the phase would pass. Once the first shock of freedom was over, the boy would take the good things he'd learned from his family life and find a new equilibrium of his own. It was obvious that, at the moment, Marco rejected his former life completely and so it was unlikely that he would be able to find this balance straight away. He even rejected his own name, and made everyone – even at home – call him by his second name, Giovanni. Marta of course defended him savagely. In her efforts to defend and justify her brother, she recalled episodes of repression and described a whole way of life that would have seemed absurd to anyone who hadn't actually lived through it. And in the process, she was able to recognise the reasons for her own revolt.

Franco rejected what our memories implied. He said that he had always acted for the good of his children and had tried to protect them from accidents or illness. The only thing he felt he could admit was that he'd loved and spoilt them too much, he'd given so generously that now they didn't know what they wanted and that was their real trouble. I remembered how everyone used to say that we spoiled the children, but I don't think children are spoilt by receiving gifts they don't even want. The presents had been an attempt to compensate them: we'd deprived them of so much and then we'd tried to cover up our anxiety and our guilt. I myself admitted to buying them presents on occasions when, instead of giving them space to live, I'd followed Franco's orders to stop them moving, running, making friends and had collaborated in keeping them like rare blooms under glass or exotic birds in a gilded cage. The doctor was extremely discreet in his role, and left us perfectly free to talk as we wished. However, he used to defend Franco because he seemed the weakest. Perhaps he was right to do so, since the father figure needed to recover some strength. But it seemed that this father figure could only recover strength at the expense of the mother figure. In other words, I had to accept a secondary position and give up any claim to running my own life. I had to offer my children a more 'feminine' image of myself. By this the doctor meant more coy, more simpering and with more frivolous interests. I should be gentler, more motherly – and more resigned.

If this had been the real road to recovery for Marta, I

would have tried to cooperate. I did in fact make some awkward attempts to comply with the doctor's advice. But the more I tried, the worse Marta got. She must have been obscurely aware of the fact that here lay the great divide between her fate and Marco's. She must have felt that the independence that she demanded for Marco should by rights have been hers too. If there were no discrimination against one sex, that independence would be the natural starting point for personal growth, as long as the family allowed all its members to develop their full potential without prejudice. But Marta's consciousness of all this was instinctive and she had no theoretical language with which to express her demands. And the immediate consequence of this was a relapse into total anorexia.

It was nearly Christmas and I promised Marta we'd have great festivities. I took her out Christmas shopping to keep her busy and then, since it was too cold to be out all the time, we started making paper chains and coloured balls. We made a beautiful Christmas crib, the best we'd ever done, really creative. And because Barbie was still a focal point, still symbolically living the life that Marta longed for, we made the doll some dresses and bought her a fiancé. Then we decided they should live together and we set about making them a house. We bought wood and a hammer and nails and we made a two-storey house with an attic and two rooms each side, on a base two metres by one metre twenty. We painted it inside and out: we painted the rooms, balconies, windows and covered stairway. Then we began to make the furniture, and we made wardrobes with drawers and mirrors, desks, upholstered armchairs and sofas, curtains and lamp-shades and everything you need in a real house, even lights. Everyone who came to see us was amazed and delighted by it. And Barbie and her boyfriend lived out their lives in there, moving from one room to the next and doing all sorts of things. But although this helped Marta to focus on the future, nothing in the present seemed to do her any good. Christmas Eve arrived, when the big festive meal takes place, and Marta couldn't bear to miss this dinner, which had always been a magic time at our house. She thought up a menu for herself: one olive, one water biscuit, one rolled anchovy, one caper.

I had promised her that we would invite Luciano and his brother and that we'd play all the traditional Christmas games. But at the last minute, only Luciano could come and they didn't play games, they just sat, embarrassed, under the coloured balls and pretty streamers, not knowing what to do. I cooked the huge traditional meal, aware that only a fraction of it would actually get eaten and aware also that Marta had eaten nothing since the previous lunchtime so as to be able to eat her tiny portion.

Franco and I stayed in the kitchen, and the atmosphere as we waited for the meal to be cooked was heavy. Indeed, when Annuccia – who'd been close to me all those weeks – dropped in to see me, I burst into tears and clung to her, sobbing, because I knew we were slipping backwards and this time I didn't know what to do. It seemed as if there were no more options, and I felt worn out and incapable of fighting any longer.

Nevertheless, we did our best to make that meal gay and hopeful, and pretended not to notice how little food Marta was eating. Most of the food finished up in the bin because we were in no state to eat much of that festive food either. Then we cleared up and sat around the table to play games – cards, tombola and so on – until it was nearly midnight. As twelve o'clock drew near we took the lighted candles and the baby Jesus from the crib and walked around the whole house, as we did every year, singing carols, until, when midnight struck, we placed the baby in his manger and then gave out the presents that lay under the Christmas tree.

On Christmas day all Marta ate was one mouthful of roast lamb. I felt desperate, and I decided to take her to my parents' house in Foggia for Boxing day, while Franco went to his parents' for lunch with Marco. My mother, who had left our house a fortnight before, and my brothers' families went to great lengths to make us feel welcome. But at lunch Marta refused everything except a tiny piece of cutlet, and then said she wanted to go out with me for an ice cream.

It was snowy weather and a cold north wind was blowing. Off I went with Marta in her short skirt and leather jacket, leaving the whole family horrified. We wandered under the leaden sky like two shadows, through the deserted streets, beneath the sad, dripping trees, and ate an ice cream in one of the few bars that were open. The cold ice went down like razors on to our empty stomachs and froze our numb bodies. We stayed out until it was almost time to go home and then we went to say goodbye to our relations. My mother saw how near to breaking point we were and she cried bitterly.

By now Marta was right back where she'd been a few weeks ago, and weighed thirty-one kilos. She only rose from her own bed to come and snuggle up to me in mine. And I lay there, without any more will to fight, resigned to meet the same fate as Marta. Franco and Marco moved around us, silent and helpless.

One afternoon Franco's parents came to see us. I got up to greet them. Then my father-in-law started: he declared that he'd always known we'd come to a sticky end. How could it be otherwise, he asked, when I hadn't done what a mother should do? A mother has to look after her children, she has to give all her time to them – whereas I had gone out to work and, not content with that, I'd even taken to writing. Actually I hadn't written for a long time, and I hadn't been able to teach for months. I didn't reply. I went back to lie next to Marta and they went on talking about me. Before they left they came into the bedroom to say goodbye. I got up and pointed to Marta, who lay there, weak and motionless.

My mother-in-law tried to comfort me: 'You'll have to resign yourself, my child. We can't expect all our children to live. I lost a child too – he was the best one, the most intelligent and good-looking one – and I couldn't do anything about it.'

I'm sure she meant well. She was trying to cheer me up because she knew we really had done everything we could and I must have looked terrible. But her words were like a whiplash to me. I said it was different for her: her son died in an accident and she really couldn't have done anything. But it wasn't like that for me, because I knew that we had killed Marta, and I was her mother, so I had to fight to the bitter end to try and save her from death. And I added that all our troubles had started when we moved here, to this town.

Instead of welcoming us lovingly, they had always attacked us, they had turned Franco against me and made our lives a misery. And I said all this was Franco's fault too, because he'd lost his confidence in me and hassled the life out of me, he'd prevented me from being the sort of mother I wanted to be to my children, stopped me from doing what I should have done for them. And now, I said, Teresa's in a mess – and it's because of your egoism and your bad advice and now she's lost her children and doesn't know what to do.

While I ranted, Franco wrung his hands. I turned to him and said it was time he chose – me or his mother? His old family or this new one he'd helped to heap troubles upon? And in front of his mother Franco put his arms round me and said, this one, this is my family. His mother and father went away in tears.

Of course, it was very unfair to say all those things to Franco's mother. What I said was true, but I had ignored all the circumstances that had led her to act as she had done. She had always meant well, and it wasn't her fault if she had created pain and sorrow. On the other hand, I was so prostrated with grief, everything seemed so lost, that I couldn't help pouring out my feelings. It was a great liberation: I felt a weight lift inside me, and I seemed to find new, unsuspected energy. Next morning I spoke to Marta with great clarity and decision:

'Listen, you know that if you carry on like this, you'll die. Everyone's beginning to tell us we should resign ourselves to your fate – they say there's no hope. I could give up the struggle and take you back into hospital. In fact, if I can't do anything else for my own daughter, then it's my last duty to take you back there and I'll do it. But is that the life you want? Don't you want to fight for a life that's worth living? Don't you want to grow strong, don't you want to be in control of yourself and your destiny, so you can do what you want to do, so you can fight to make other people understand what you have understood? Don't you want to help to free other people from the oppression that you have felt yourself? Each one of us is small, it's true, but we can each call up unimaginable energies and it's worth living just for that, even if you suffer. It's worth it, it's better than being crushed, better than giving in without a fight and dying, or living a slave's life which is just like death. Now, you have to choose: if you are weak, if you can't fight, then go to your fate – death or slavery. But if you can suffer and fight, you have to grow strong, you have to put all your energy into life, with no half measures.'

At these words the chains which had imprisoned Marta's will to live fell apart – at last! The floodgates opened, and in her excited response I heard echoes of all the various themes we'd searched through in all those months, without ever finding the thread, and I knew for sure that Marta had chosen to live. She'd chosen to live as a real person, to search for others – she wanted to fight and break the chains and barriers so as to get her own self and her own life back. No one and nothing could stop her now. Finally the doors of the future opened to her after all this time she'd spent outside unable to open them. And her anorexia, her extreme gesture, ceased; it was no longer necessary. After she'd got all this off her chest, a doubt suddenly struck her: hadn't everyone said that anorexia was incurable? That is certainly how she had seen her illness – like a blind alley that leads nowhere except to death.

'Nonsense,' I said quickly. 'As long as the anorexia lasts, it can only lead to death, but as soon as you decide to fight for life, it disappears. And isn't that what you've done? You've decided to fight and suffer so as to seek a better, more authentic life for yourself and others?'

Now all that remained was for her to get used to eating again, so that her stomach could gradually start working properly. And the rest of her body too – now she would begin to see it as a precious and vital ally which she would learn to love and use, a vehicle for all the pleasures of life yet to be discovered. Maybe it sounds theatrical, but we had become the characters in a drama, and the play was none the worse for our very private performance. Everybody's life is a drama, after all, and it's only because people don't always stop to think about it that they don't realise what they are living through. And they act their part all the more naturally because they are unaware of the stage. We had not felt the need of an audience. We'd played out our drama, day by day, behind closed doors and all that had been visible to the outsider was no doubt our haunted expressions, for anyone who felt the desire to decipher their significance.

From that moment on Marta gradually got better. Of course there were many different phases to her recovery and several pauses; there were times when she was enthusiastic and other times when she felt too despondent to carry on. But there was a tacit understanding between us that she would try to free her real self and I would try to support and encourage her and defend her against attacks from the environment. Everybody else, including all our relations, breathed a sigh of relief when they heard that Marta was on the mend, and promptly forgot the whole business. However, after a while they decided that there was still something wrong and they seemed irritated by us, as if they wanted to say: 'But why can't you be normal?'

Normal. What does normal mean? Somebody who stays within the norm? Couldn't they see that we had left the norm behind for ever because for us the norm now meant death? We were different. We were different because we were looking for a more honest way of life, for a lifestyle that would satisfy our deepest needs, even if that meant alienation from everyone else, for a relationship with the outside world that we didn't find castrating. Being different meant rethinking everything – it meant our own cultural revolution. That is why we gradually changed and developed as human beings.

But who – out of the four of us – really made this effort? Marta did and she continues to do so, because the struggle is a never-ending one. It's like a chain reaction: once it's set in motion it won't stop. I made the effort, too, and I continue to do so, even though Marta often notices the old mentality tripping me up. I try to break through these bonds, and I also try to help Marta see when she's caught up in the rigid thinking that is the hallmark of our society, weighed down as it is with its own past. But what about Franco and Marco?

Here's the rub! I am Franco's wife and I love him too much to abandon him to his fate. And I'm Marco's mother and I love him just as much as I love Marta: as long as I live I want to be there for him too, even if he is often hostile and rejecting towards me. The split in our family widened during Marta's gradual recovery and it was just as painful for all of us as the illness itself had been. Because the split is an illness of the family both as a unit and at the individual level. It affects all the personal interaction that makes up the fabric of our daily lives. It destroys our energy and, because I act as mediator, all the tension unloads on to me, draining my energy faster than anyone else's. I never cease to be amazed at Franco's capacity for putting things behind him and carrying on regardless, forgetting everything he's learned and going back to the same old life.

When we realised that the doctor had led us in the wrong direction, we paid his fee and said goodbye to him. He had tried to restore us to a state of 'normality' where we would accept society's norms unquestioningly – even down to the fashion in clothes. We were different before we began, and our goal was to become conscious of our difference so that we could continue on our path, creating new ways of relating to other people. We needed this new awareness so that we could understand others and make them understand us without having to resort to compromises. A new phase began for us: the real identity of each member of the family was now laid bare for the others to see, and we could no longer hide behind conventions and formulas. Franco was the only one of the four who still believed that the moral values and patterns of behaviour that he'd learned from his father were the only possible guidelines for an honest and well regulated life. We three felt like wild horses: we each sought our freedom eagerly. No doubt we made mistakes and certainly we sometimes went too far – but that was understandable.

It upset me that Marco listened to his father instead of thinking for himself, because when Franco felt really threatened he would appeal to innate male superiority. He would label us women mad and presumptuous for demanding the same level of independence as the men. I tried to reason with Marco, but he attacked me and his sister as if we were enemies instead of allies. Perhaps at first I was too busy helping Marta to rebuild her life – or demolish her old life – and I didn't do enough to help Marco. I ought to have helped him see straight away that the demolition process was in his interests too.

One of the first things we dismantled was the Barbie myth. Marta finally realised that Barbie was a symbol of the false emancipation of women. She represented the insidious invitation of the consumer society to women, its attempt to divert women's demands into channels which are harmless and non-threatening to the system. Barbie was just a middle-class girl with money in her pocket. Maybe she'd earned it herself, but she and her fiancé spent all their money on consumer goods – on a life of luxury and endless frivolity. Barbie was happy in her golden cage: she had no problems, no social awareness, no doubts. She represented a completely self-centred life.

When Marta realised what a serious threat to her search for truth and freedom that golden cage represented, she took Barbie's house to pieces and threw the whole thing away. Barbie became just another ornament in her bedroom, along with her other trinkets. Marta dressed her in the same imaginative way that she herself had begun to dress. I spent time with Marta each day analysing our lives, and every day she brought to this dialogue all kinds of elements from her intense emotional relationships and from her observations of her own behaviour and other people's.

But I also took time to go over my own past life now that I felt able to decipher it properly. Now that I reflected on my experience, I saw that Nestore had tried to make me feel guilty about my children. In helping me to retrace my origins and Franco's, he had asked me to recognise that our mothers were guilty. Indeed, we had recognised that our respective mothers had not given us what we needed – they could never have given it because they too were conditioned by their own upbringing. This made me feel the same guilt, especially over Marco, whom I had deprived of love in my desire to be impartial with the two children. And I had done it at a time when he was too small to claim his proper share of my exclusive attention. I felt guilty and perhaps my sense of guilt had played a part in Marta's story. After all, I was certainly responsible in part for her illness.

In the light of our experience with Marta, I really wanted to take a good look at this guilt-producing process on which psychoanalytic therapy – and indeed the whole Freudian vision – is based, at least in its current form. Nestore and our other doctor, as well as the whole Psychiatric Hospital team had all tried to convince me that the mother is always wrong: our mothers, who had lived according to the rules of traditional society, were wrong – and I was wrong, even more wrong, because I had rejected those rules and tried to bring up my children without regard for sex roles.

I had a very strong impression that all this therapy was designed not so much to extricate human beings from difficulties by an unprejudiced search for the real traps, but to defend and maintain the power system by all available means – including the most violent and ugly.

Official, institutional psychotherapy (unlike the revolutionary, alternative anti-Freudian therapy which emerged a little later and which I hadn't heard of at the time) certainly defends male culture against it own alienating consequences. We are living in the final, extreme stages of that culture, and its affects are everywhere.

I traced my personal prehistory back and discovered some elements there which gave me the analytical key to other subterranean depths where the prehistory of the whole human race lies buried like a pile of useless and forgotten artefacts. I too had lived through a period of penis envy and I too had grown up with the marks of castration on me. This sense of having been castrated was woven into my very being, and it was the source of my anguish – it had made me what I was. Now I found it easy to go back to my earliest memories and even to recapture my childhood dreams and interpret them properly.

I had always remembered one particular recurring nightmare that I had had since I was two. I checked it with mother, to whom I had recounted this nightmare when I was a girl, pointing it out to her as the first sign of my emerging consciousness. The scene took place in the house where I was born and which we left a few months later. It was night time and I was woken by a strange wimpering from my newborn brother. When he was born my little iron bed had been moved from my mother's side of the bed on the right to the left, next to my father. The baby in his wicker cradle now occupied the space next to my mother. That whimpering, quickly silenced by my mother as she picked him up to feed him, woke me out of my sleep. I opened my eyes and saw a reddish light which filled the room and sent great, dark shadows across the ceiling. The shadows were familiar and friendly and I wasn't afraid of them. But I was afraid when I saw in front of my eyes a multitude of little things no bigger than a finger. I described these to my mother as 'dead man's bones' – the name of a sort of traditional marzipan cake we ate in those parts on All Souls' Day, shaped just like a little bone. Perhaps those cakes had their orign in ancient funeral rites when people ate part of the corpse to preserve the life of their dead in their own bodies. Of course, my mother had never been able to explain this dream to me, and maybe I'd never tried to interpret it. I was content to see in this experience the beginnings of my sense of the closeness of death, something I'd always felt. This sense of death was made up of fear but also desire, as if I'd never felt at home amongst other living beings.

But now that I had recovered that other memory – of myself being sent away from the house so as not to disturb my mother while she fed my brother – the significance of this dream seemed clear to me. Those little bones were my baby brother's penis, which was paraded in front of my eyes all the time because it was high summer and my thoughtful mother dressed him in a little vest and nothing else so as to keep him cool in our sultry climate. I would never have dreamt of envying him that little thing once I'd notice my own lack of it, had it not been the object of gratified contemplation by the whole family. Gathered around him in a circle, they would make admiring remarks:

'He really is a beautiful boy! A real boy!'

And it didn't take me long to discover that what made him a boy was just that single anatomical difference from me. Perhaps that wouldn't have bothered me, but then I saw that all my singing and dancing and imitations – which had so far kept everyone's attention on me and won me kisses and caresses – were to no avail, because my baby brother, just by exhibiting this little thing he possessed, held everyone's attention. I was relegated to the background, and no one took any more notice of me. And if I did anything to get some attention, I was rebuked:

'Don't you realise you're a little girl? It's not nice for little girls to do things like that!'

This business of being a little girl now seemed to imply inferiority, almost as if I were a second-class individual who was not permitted the freedom of expression reserved for first-class individuals – for males in other words. I felt exuberantly alive and I just couldn't come to terms with this. So I rebelled: I carried on behaving as if I had the same rights I had enjoyed before, when I was an only child and everyone had accepted me unconditionally. And my punishment was swift: I was sent away so that I wouldn't bother everyone. There was photographic proof that I had bothered them. Our family album contains a brief sequence of photos: in the first one, Nino, aged about three months, is sitting back like a king on an armchair with his sceptre clearly visible between his fat, bandy little legs, and there am I next to him, looking at him – in fact looking at his sceptre. What can I have done while my father was turning the film on? The angelic smile on Nino's face has turned into a desperate wail in the next photo, and I am caught in the act of running away. Had I tried to steal his sceptre? Maybe.

But that sceptre was irremovable. And it was my death sentence, because it confirmed that I was no longer allowed to express my vitality and no one had time for me, no matter what I did or said. That's why in my nightmare my brother's penis merged with a death symbol, and that's why I was afraid. I was afraid and I cried, and my father reached out a hand and rocked me back to sleep. Maybe that's when I first became really aware of his presence and perhaps it was then that I began to turn to him instead of my mother. Would I have felt penis envy, I wondered, if I hadn't had tangible and concrete evidence that the lack of a penis meant increasingly severe restrictions to my own free development?

I had every opportunity to see what a big difference there was between me and the boy children, because three boys were born, one after the other, each with his own sceptre, and my mother's attention was completely taken up by her new babies. She no longer had any time or energy to see to me, and my exile at my kind grandmother's house lasted throughout my childhood and puberty, until the bombard-ment and my father's death.

I had been mutilated, prevented from being what my nature intended – a person with as much right to self-expression as my brothers. If I suffered from a castration complex, it was not an inevitable part of being a woman, it was because, as a woman, the world judged me to be worth less and deserving of less than my brothers, who had the good luck to belong to the category of first-class people. The feelings of envy were the natural consequence of the process of castration.

And now I was also able to interpret another recurring dream from my childhood. I started having this dream when my family already numbered six. I often dreamed that I was in an empty room where there were nothing but a black lacquered piano. My mother sat at the keyboard and played – she played for me alone and I really enjoyed the music. Right in the middle, a beautiful, golden-haired, cherubic baby boy appeared opposite me, at the other end of the room. He stopped at the other side of the piano and looked at me with a scornful, triumphant smile. Then he reached out his arm and hand as if he were about to crush me. Then the whole scene changed grotesquely before my eyes: my mother disappeared and the cherubic baby multiplied as if there were a hundred mirrors. That outstretched hand grew huge and reached nearer and nearer to me, threateningly. The piano changed shape too and lengthened until it turned into a coffin.

That was the extent of my castration – I felt a death sentence hanging over my head. That's how a person feels if their life force is repressed and their freedom of growth is restricted. Why would any woman suffer from penis envy or castration complexes if she could live a free life on a par with men?

But to help a woman recognise the feelings she's experi-enced and yet hide the real reasons from her – that is an attempt to get her to accept her subordinate position as if it were a natural consequence of her biology. It is an attempt to lead her quietly back into the flock. And that is what they'd tried to do to me and my daughter. We were already involved in our own deconditioning process – an irreversible process – and yet they had tried to recondition us.

Now, at last, I felt able to face my relationship with Franco, and my own sexuality. Gradually, as I had freed myself from the inhibitions that surrounded me as a person, I had discovered that I enjoyed making love and that I wasn't passive but creative, expansive, tender, and that I wanted to bring out Franco's real potential and his real warmth. I wanted to play with his plump but agile body, tease him and draw him out – with a new sense of adventure, as if we'd never been together before. I was surprised at his reactions. He was delighted and he seemed freed from the prejudices that I had once felt to be powerful inhibiting factors to my own spontaneity, as if it were a fault to let him see my pleasure or to show any initiative. Nevertheless, he seemed to take refuge in me instead of unfolding, as if his supreme desire was to return to the womb. And so the more I developed as a woman, the more he forced me back into my role as mother. I don't think it was an Oedipus complex, as Marta's doctor claimed. He thought Franco identified me with his mother. This seemed to me a superficial and clumsy explanation and my intuition told me that it was not distorted sexuality that gave rise to his behaviour, but an existential block. Here was a person whose natural growth and development had somehow been inhibited, and this block now held him a prisoner so that the source of all his responses was this primal pain.

I thought back over the various stages of our early relationship. We had always felt an enormously powerful mutual attraction, and we'd both felt excited by each other when we first met. I had looked to him like an unsophisticated schoolgirl and to me he had seemed a wild rebel, full of all sorts of real passions that made his small, lean body vibrate. Together we'd learned to kiss and touch each other and he used to cover my whole body with his soft mouth and hot hands, feverishly evoking my own desire. On this level, our relationship was perfect and it was one of the basic reasons for our tenacity in the face of so much family opposition.

We didn't make love completely because we were both full of moral standards that prevented such a thing, and although Franco tried hard enough, he always said he was pleased to see that I was firm enough to stop him, even though I too trembled with desire. It never entered my head that my duty could be otherwise and I always resisted his attempts, energetically defending the gateway of my fortress. On the other hand, we were open enough with each other to keep a careful track of my menstrual cycle for months before our marriage so that we'd be able to make love without any precautions, at a time when there would be no danger of my getting pregnant. We had decided not to have any children at first so that we could pay off all the debts we'd incurred when we set up house.

I was the one who furnished the house and I was a little disappointed that Franco didn't seem very interested in what was going on. But he said he didn't know the first thing about household furnishings and that he had confidence in my taste. I was so happy to be creating a home that I didn't take much notice.

So we were quite unprepared for what happened on our wedding night. I was excited but not frightened. Franco was tense and nervous. He suddenly forgot all the erotic games we were so good at and behaved as if he were taking an exam in front of a demanding and intransigent examiner and, for the first time, his penis hung limp and lifeless. He suddenly had an attack of stomach cramp and began to sweat profusely. Finally he vomited up our evening meal of beer and meringue. We decided it was indigestion and gave up for that night.

The next day we visited Teresa in Milan and Franco confided the story of the previous night to her. She reassured us, saying her brother had always suffered from these sudden, bad stomach upsets. She thought they were due to his sensitive nature and advised me to treat him with hot water bottles and herb tea with plenty of sugar. However, when she got Franco on his own she put him on his guard against me. She thought I seemed too free and self-assured, too strong and assertive a character and said I was probably the main cause of his sudden impotence. She advised Franco to curb me, make sure I knew my place, otherwise he'd end up like one of those famous husbands whose wife wears the trousers. Now her theory didn't really suit Franco's personality. He was a mild man, who tended to relate to the motherly side of women. But he accepted her warning uncritically. He too was sure that the only way out of the confrontation with me was to show himself and me that he was the stronger, dominant partner. Only this victory would re-establish his virility: as long as we faced each other on equal terms, he would never be able to express his sexuality.

I tried to reason with him because I wanted to preserve my rights as a person. I remembered how I'd fought for my independence. But Franco quickly assumed an attitude of irrational violence: he cut out the talk and used pure physical strength against the enemy, with no holds barred. At this point I felt it was beneath my dignity to fight back: it would have turned into a ridiculous scuffle and, after all, we were married. I had sworn – without really understanding what it meant – to respect my husband's conjugal rights and submit to him. Unless I wanted to force Franco to rape me, I had to give in, castrate myself and bear it. Now I understood what had been celebrated at the altar: it was unconditional surrender. It was only after two months of resistance and failed attempts that Franco was convinced that he'd broken me in, that I was resigned to the unconditional surrender and the annihilation of my personality for the exaltation of his. Then the marriage was consummated, his penis started working again, and he penetrated me – marching into his conquered territory. I immediately conceived Marta.

One of the first formal acts which put the seal on Franco's hard won supremacy – enhanced by my self-sacrifice – was the brass plate he went and ordered and then triumphantly put up outside our front door. I say 'our' front door, but I was horrified to see that I did not figure at all on this plate – as if I no longer existed. It read 'Prof.', followed by Franco's name and surname. That was it. That was the residence of the new lord and master. Whoever else his master had taken into his home to reproduce him, to serve him sexually, to cook and clean, to work and bring home money, was of no interest: I was so-and-so's wife, and there was no need for my name to appear next to his. I was a second-class person, a slave captured in war, who might attain some rights at some future date if she was a loyal, dedicated, hard-working, tireless, self-sacrificing, humble servant, just like the deserving slaves who were occasionally freed by their owners as a reward for long years of service. So I did not return Franco's child-like triumphant smile when he showed me his door plate. It ratified his power and my slavery.

The years that followed were soaked in my slave's sweat and blood. I was born free and I fought for my breathing space so as not to suffocate under the drudgery. I turned inwards and tried to survive by calling on my mental resources and by living a creative inner life. But I was always jerked back to reality by Franco, whose own fear of castration and need to dominate reappeared whenever he saw my desire for freedom surfacing. Franco grasped the nuptial knot and pulled, and over the years that knot tightened and almost choked me and my children, as I've described, despite his stubborn conviction that he did it for our own good. And the knot choked him, too, in the end: that's why, in the final analysis, I felt sorry for him and fought to liberate him along with the rest of us.

Because how could I be satisfied at this point with the explanation that I'd castrated Franco? When I'd always loved him and wanted him and longed for a complete relationship with him, one that was founded on mutual respect? No, the damage to his personality must have happened way back in time. I had always perceived a split between Franco's exuberant, rich, generous nature, his passion for justice and human rights – and his cowardly, unconditional surrender to power, whatever form it took. This pattern of behaviour made him insecure, fragile and vulnerable towards anyone who had power. And it wasn't just the physical fear experienced by a man who feels unequal to a contest of strength. I know small men who can challenge giants.

His fear was a deep, ancestral fear, the fear that penetrates the spirit of a child born into a regime of violent and despotic terror. The child learns not to resist, he learns to bend his will humbly and obediently in order to survive. And the person who struck holy terror into Franco was his father, who was now an old man, but still powerful. He had always laid down the law in Franco's family and no one ever opposed his wishes. All through his childhood and adolescence, Franco had feared his father's terrible, cruel punishments, and now as a grown man he feared his judgment. And so he was incapable of making any independent decisions that deviated from the moral values he'd been brought up with. Yet he'd been a far more affectionate and kindly father than his own father had been. But when it was no longer a matter of affection, when it came to the rules for bringing up children, the gap in his personality became enormous. Franco had always tried to lay down the law without realising that his rules could not be upheld without the reinforcement of a terrifying, internalised father figure. No doubt that's why his children loved him more than they feared him. But in his desire to enforce his rules, he had often used this love to blackmail them into obedience; his own childhood obedience had been obtained by means of violence and oppression.

This only worked while Marta and Marco were too small to think for themselves. As soon as they were old enough, they began to question his role as educator. Then he blamed me and said I was the cause of failure because I had presumed to use my woman's brain instead of carrying out my wifely duties of slave-cum-jailor.

It was only by chance that I found out something very important, something which helped to throw light on this final problem.

Teresa had recently decided to move back north. There was nothing to keep her here now that her daughter had given up hope of finding work and settling down here. Liliana had managed to find a good, satisfying job in Milan, in spite of the high unemployment there. She must have reached a new level of maturity because before she left she confessed something to me that she hadn't told anyone else. She couldn't face telling her mother: it was a secret she had lived with since early childhood, something which had ruined all those years. It was very hard for her to get the truth out, but she finally managed to tell me what she had lived through in her maternal grandparents' strict household when she'd

132

been sent there on holiday as a small child. Her mother often sent her to stay there by herself, perhaps as a peace offering to her own abandoned mother, so that the old lady could enjoy her granddaughter's company.

Her grandmother gave her plenty of attention and showered her with little presents. So did her grandfather – but his attentions were of quite a different nature. As she grew older his pleasure in her young body became more and more pronounced, and he used to touch her lasciviously and do things to her which were quite explicit, although she was too little and too naive to recognise the danger or defend herself from him. This had gone on right up to the beginning of her adolescence, and she had never dared to rebel or say anything about it to her mother, because she knew Teresa sent her south to make up for her own absence.

Liliana had serious guilt feelings about this incestuous relationship. She had suffered it as something to be lived through, something she had colluded with and which it was impossible to get away from. And she had also suffered serious consequences in her own natural sexual development: her sense of guilt had made it difficult for her to feel anything for men outside the family group. Thus she had fallen in love with her young uncle, Franco's youngest brother, who also tended to respond to her sexually, and even with her own brother. Sergio had a period of intimacy with her but quickly turned to other women, leaving Liliana acutely jealous. She couldn't help being jealous of any woman her brother loved, including the one who later became her sister-in-law.

This had been the powerful stimulus that had prompted Liliana to get pregnant by the first man she met. She didn't care about him; she felt as if she'd finally committed the long-desired incest with her brother and it was as if she were having his child. Now that she had become conscious of all this, she had decided to burn her bridges and forget this family of her mother's which had done her nothing but harm. She hoped her mother would find the courage to forget her native city and return north as well. She added that she had noticed for some time that the old man, far from abandoning his unhealthy desires, had turned his attention to the other

133

granddaughters, and she believed they were all caught in the same situation. This was one more reason for getting out now: she didn't want him to start on her own baby daughter.

This shocking revelation brought back to me an episode that had happened when we first moved here.

I had not yet found a woman to look after the children while Franco and I were at work, and my father-in-law kindly offered to look after the house and the children. I accepted gratefully and without a qualm. One evening, not long after the beginning of term, as I was undressing Marta I found long, red marks all down her body. I was alarmed and I asked her what had happened. Marta said she didn't know, and no matter how many questions I asked her – including whether her grandfather had done it – she said no, she just didn't know. I was very frightened and confused, and when I thought about it carefully of course I realised that it must have been Franco's father. I tried to imagine him suddenly getting excited by the sight of the little girl's body – a woman in miniature – and touching her to the extent of leaving marks on her tender flesh. But I found it so hard to reconcile such a scene with the stern, upright, moralistic and respect-able father figure that I put the horrific thought right out of my mind. I was tempted on various occasions to say something to Franco about it, but our communication was then at an all-time low. Franco ruled the house with a rod of iron and anyway, he had such a reverent attitude towards the old patriarch that I couldn't formulate any sort of accusation even in my own head. I gave up trying to think about it; all I wanted to do was forget and I can see now how a repressed mind, deprived of liberty, is incapable of understanding or seeing the truth. It can even block out memory. I engaged the first woman the employment agency sent me and asked her to start work the next day. And I never left the children alone with their grandfather again, although Franco's brothers continued to do so; they were sure that nobody could look after their children as well as their wonderful, loving grandparents.

I only remembered this episode years later when Marta was ill and I was trying to work out the underlying reasons for her condition. Then I did talk to Franco about it. He could hardly believe his ears and acted as if I'd invented the whole story. Nevertheless, he plucked up his courage and went and asked his father if he'd ever . . . But the old man's reaction was terrifying: how dare his son think such a thing? I must have gone mad, I'd lost my reason! Franco reproached me for that scene with his father and told me to stop blaming his family and take a good look at myself – I was the one who'd undermined his authority. And he enjoined me not to go telling the doctor stories like that because it wasn't fair to ruin the family reputation. I did ask Marta about it again, to see if she remembered that particular episode or any other episode of violence on her grandfather's part. But she couldn't remember anything at all, and even when the whole story came out, nothing of the sort came back to her.

I saw the whole picture now: the old patriarch was the very incarnation of the age old violence that has been perpetrated on generations of sons and daughters in the name of the sacred, inviolable right of males to dominate their families. The sons are all castrated and subjected to the iron law of discipline and duty, cowed by the violence of the father's repression; the daughters are enslaved to *jus primae noctis*, that ancient heritage, and their submission is so complete that they suffer their own violation in silence, against their own interests, because the fear of punishment discourages any rebellion.

Here then is the individual who had wrought such havoc with Franco's life, and with the lives of all his other children and his wife. He was himself a victim of a distorted, centuries-old conception of human relations. And who knows what experiences he had undergone to make him what he was; to ensure his allegiance to the double standard morality which allows men to crush people's wills with their castrating, guilt producing laws and yet permits unrestricted areas of self indulgence with exclusive rights and no limits.

How would Franco react if he could see the real face of his father? Would he be able to stand the shock, in the psychologically fragile state he was in now?

I talked to the children about it. They had to know the truth because it would help them to see the real Franco after all the scorn and contempt he'd suffered. It had helped me to realise how much I really loved him and how much we could still give each other – if only we could help him see the truth. The children and I agreed that I would try to find the right moment to tell him.

That moment came when Franco's family was in a great crisis. Teresa took her things and left to join her children. She went on tiptoe, without saying goodbye to anyone, not even to her mother. Perhaps she hadn't the courage to tell her that she was abandoning her again, and in her old age, when perhaps the old lady really did need comfort and help. My mother-in-law was devastated; she wept for Teresa as if she were dead and couldn't understand how she'd had the heart to leave without even putting her arms round her mother for the last time. Her sons and daughters-in-law and grandchildren, who couldn't understand it themselves, stood awkwardly around her as she sat with her grief, not knowing how to comfort her.

It was in this atmosphere that it suddenly came naturally to me, one night, to tell him. It came easily because he had turned to me for comfort in a moment of hurt and pain. I had never loved him so much as I did at that moment. And I wanted him – his real self as he could be once he'd found the courage to sever his umbilical cord. Perhaps the child in him might have died then if he hadn't had someone there to heal the wound, someone who'd been wounded too but who had come through it all and now stood waiting for him – a whole person offering herself to him in complete freedom. This is who we are.